Missio Dei and the United States

Toward a Faithful United Methodist Witness

Study Guide

HIGHER EDUCATION & MINISTRY
General Board of Higher Education and Ministry

THE UNITED METHODIST CHURCH

Missio Dei and the United States: Toward a Faithful United Methodist Witness, Study Guide

The General Board of Higher Education and Ministry leads and serves The United Methodist Church in the recruitment, preparation, nurture, education, and support of Christian leaders—lay and clergy—for the work of making disciples of Jesus Christ for the transformation of the world. Its vision is that a new generation of Christian leaders will commit boldly to Jesus Christ and be characterized by intellectual excellence, moral integrity, spiritual courage, and holiness of heart and life. The General Board of Higher Education and Ministry of The United Methodist Church serves as an advocate for the intellectual life of the church. The Board's mission embodies the Wesleyan tradition of commitment to the education of laypersons and ordained persons by providing access to higher education for all persons.

Missio Dei and the United States: Toward a Faithful United Methodist Witness, Study Guide

ISBN 978-1-945935-26-8

18 19 20 21 22 23 24 25 26 27—10 9 8 7 6 5 4 3 2 1

Manufactured in the United States of America

HIGHER EDUCATION & MINISTRY
General Board of Higher Education and Ministry
THE UNITED METHODIST CHURCH

Contents

Introduction

Kim Cape

General Secretary, General Board
of Higher Education and Ministry,
The United Methodist Church

t is still dark when students begin their journey in Juarez, Mexico, walking across the international bridge to attend the Lydia Patterson Institute in El Paso, Texas, a high school owned by the South Central Jurisdiction of The United Methodist Church. Eighty percent of the four hundred Lydia Patterson students make this journey every school day. Some even have a two-hour bus ride before they start their walk across the bridge. They wear their school uniforms, laughing and chatting in both Spanish and English. Their classrooms are state of the art with laptops and teachers who use the latest innovative teaching methods. It is clear that teachers come to Lydia Patterson not for the pay, because these teacher salaries are much less than what public school teachers earn, but because they are committed to the mission of providing an excellent education to the poorest border children. Founded in 1913 by a Methodist laywoman (Lydia Patterson) who wanted Mexican children to read, Lydia Patterson was one of the first schools in the United States to focus on English as a second language.

Most students are on scholarship and participate in a work-study program at the school. Eager to learn, 95 percent of students at Lydia Patterson graduate, and 98 percent of those who graduate attend college. It is clear these students understand that education is their means of lifting themselves out of the cycle of poverty and living into God's promise of fullness of life. I learned this firsthand as I sat at lunch with a student. Delia's ambition is to become an opera singer. Seeing the dedication and commitment of the students, teachers, and administrative staff, I believe that Lydia Patterson is one of the finest missions The United Methodist Church supports in the world.

Dr. Socorro de Anda, the principal of Lydia Patterson, met with the General Secretaries when we held our meeting there. She is a force of nature and left a lucrative business career to lead Lydia Patterson. After a tour of the facility, we had a frank conversation about the needs of the school and the challenges of her work. Virtually the first question Dr. de Anda raised concerned the future of The United Methodist Church and the work of the Way Forward Commission: What will happen to Lydia Patterson if the church splits and their support is withdrawn? Dr. de Anda has no voice and no vote and feels her life's work in missions is at stake, yet she continues to pray that the Way Forward Commission finds a way that does no harm.

None of us knows the future of God's mission for The United Methodist Church. None of us knows how far-reaching the consequences of our decisions will be. I invite all of us to pray that as we walk through these difficult times, we do not fail to remember that the Delias of Lydia Patterson are counting on us. I also pray that she and others like her will be able to continue to follow the call of God in their lives and that the missio Dei of The United Methodist Church will be stronger and more vibrant as a result of the Way Forward.

We believe that the church is eager for in-depth theological conversation and discernment about God's mission for us, the community of faith. This study guide invites us to love God with our minds and participate in advancing that mission. For United Methodists, loving God is not based on sentiment or transient emotion. Rather, we love by our faithful practice, our concrete actions to serve God and neighbor. This means that we act with forethought, seeking to impact and thereby transform the world by making disciples. Loving God means

Engage
for a Vibrant
Wesleyan Movement

Scott J. Jones

Resident Bishop of the Houston Episcopal
Area, The United Methodist Church

A radically changed and changing mission context provides the Wesleyan movement significant challenges and opportunities for the years ahead. The gospel of Jesus Christ is unchanging because, as Hebrews 13:8 reminds us, "Jesus Christ is the same yesterday and today and forever" (NRSV). Yet a changed culture requires a different approach to fulfilling Jesus's mandate to "make disciples of all nations" (Matt. 28:19 NRSV). This chapter summarizes the five most important changes and then discusses opportunities that present themselves to the Wesleyan movement.

1. It Is No Longer 1950

Stanley Hauerwas and William Willimon opened their 1989 book *Resident Aliens: A Provocative Christian Assessment of Culture and Ministry for People Who Know that Something Is Wrong* with these words:

> Somewhere between 1960 and 1980, an old, inadequately conceived world ended, and a fresh, new world began . . .

> When and how did we change? Although it may sound trivial, one of us is tempted to date the shift sometime on a Sunday evening in 1963. Then, in Greenville, South Carolina, in defiance of the state's time-honored blue laws, the Fox Theater opened on Sunday. Seven of us—regular attenders of the Methodist Youth Fellowship at Buncombe Street Church—made a pact to enter the front door of the church, be seen, then quietly slip out the back door and join John Wayne at the Fox.[1]

At whatever point one dates the change, it has clearly happened. For most of America's history Protestant churches have enjoyed a type of cultural establishment. It was a privileged position where Sunday mornings (and often Wednesday nights) were respected and protected for church activities. Newspapers sometimes printed sermons on their front pages. To be pastor of a church meant an assured place of leadership in the community. Those things are true no longer, and most of the culture-shaping institutions today have become increasingly indifferent or actively hostile to the Church.

2. The Enlightenment Won

Philosophical and intellectual trends began to be hostile to revelation and religion in the seventeenth century but gained significant power in the nineteenth and twentieth centuries. The focus on reason and individualism over any form of religious authority was a direct attack on the Christian church and its role in society. Over time people have proved to be less rational than philosophers assumed, and freedom has proved to be a mixed blessing. By the late twentieth century expressive individualism came to characterize the thinking of many, even those who professed a form of Christianity. One thinks of "sheilaism" as described in Robert Bellah's *Habits of the Heart*. Atheism has gained

---

1   Stanley Hauerwas and William H. Willimon, *Resident Aliens: A Provocative Christian Assessment of Culture and Ministry for People Who Know that Something Is Wrong* (Nashville: Abingdon, 1989), 15.

ground in the public square and has come to be a dominant force in the faculties of major universities. The ideas that God matters in day-to-day life and that God has revealed God's will in the Bible are simply ludicrous to the cultural elites who shape American culture today.

3. People Are Lonely

Robert Putnam's *Bowling Alone: The Collapse and Revival of American Community* remains an important analysis of how the loss of social capital has led to myriads of dysfunctions. He documents increases in divorce, depression, suicide, drug addiction, and other problems; while at the same time there has been a drastic decline in the web of relationships that give life meaning and purpose. Causes as varied as air conditioning, television, and the mass movement of women into the workforce have all contributed to the loss of social capital.

4. Populations Are Increasingly Diverse

While the world has always had a diverse human population with multiple nations, languages, ethnicities, and cultures, increased migration and greater ease of travel have brought diverse populations into much closer proximity to one another. Leaders of Houston, Texas claim theirs is the most ethnically diverse city in the United States, with over 140 languages spoken in the homes of its citizens. Estimates suggest that one-fourth of Houston's residents were born outside the United States. Many communities in the United States are experiencing an influx of Hispanic immigrants, with some estimations of eleven million persons here without documentation. A recent estimate suggests that 13 percent of Americans today were born in a different country, the highest percentage since 1910.[2] While much of this diversity is centered in cities, it has also come to characterize

---

2 Fred Dews, "What Percentage of U.S. Population Is Foreign Born?" *Brookings*, October 3, 2013, https://www.brookings.edu/blog/brookings-now/2013/10/03/what-percentage-of-u-s-population-is-foreign-born.

smaller communities where jobs for immigrants are available. Dodge City, Kansas and its surrounding Ford County has a population that is 40 percent Hispanic.

5. The World Is Flat

Thomas Friedman's important book *The World Is Flat: A Brief History of the Twenty-First Century* convincingly describes the many ways in which people are now connected globally. Digital communication technology and the ease of air travel have broken down traditional barriers of time and space. Families are connected by video conversations; people share information through social media, e-mail, and phones that provide instantaneous communication. Goods are manufactured in different countries and then shipped to other places to be assembled or sold. In order to make a living, corn farmers and cattle ranchers in the Midwest must take into account weather patterns in Brazil and currency fluctuations in China. A telephone call for service may be routed to the Philippines or India. It is truly a global economy. Global migration means that people in Chicago may have direct information about conditions in Sudan.

Institutional Challenges

These five changes pose significant institutional challenges for all Christian churches in America. Insights from three important books help clarify the organizational implications. Moisés Naím's *The End of Power* notes that there have been three revolutions changing how big organizations function.[3] The *More* revolution means people have increased resources and thus a wider array of options. The *Mentality* revolution means that people have been exposed to different belief systems and no longer must follow authorities. The *Mobility* revolution means that

---

3 Moisés Naím, *The End of Power: From Boardrooms to Battlefields and Churches to States, Why Being in Charge Isn't What It Used to Be* (New York: Basic Books, 2014), 54–65.

people move to different places and find new patterns of allegiance and relationship. The US Army had trouble with the mujhadeen in Afghanistan, and the Catholic Church had trouble with Pentecostals in Latin America. Smaller, more local, and more nimble businesses often triumphed over larger and traditionally dominant rivals.

Yuval Levin's *The Fractured Republic* describes American culture as experiencing a strong process of centralization in the middle part of the twentieth century.[4] He argues that the decades between 1930 and 1970 were an unusual time of consolidation and centralization. Beginning in 1945 the reaction set in, and the process of deconsolidation and decentralization set in. Individual freedom and expressionism took hold. America will never again have the kind of cultural cohesiveness experienced in the 1950s. While increasing freedom has empowered many, it has created a much more complicated social fabric.

 Being fruitful and faithful is more difficult now than at any time in American history.

Overall, these challenges mean that being fruitful and faithful is much more difficult now than at any time before in American history. Given such a rapidly changing and increasingly hostile context, the most important step that a church can take is to gain clarity of purpose. Patrick Lencioni's *The Advantage: Why Organizational Health Trumps Everything Else in Business* argues that creating clarity, over-communicating clarity, and reinforcing clarity are the key elements leading to effectiveness in all organizations, whether nonprofit or for-profit.[5] When an organization is clear about its purpose and then

4   Yuval Levin, *The Fractured Republic: Renewing America's Social Contract in the Age of Individualism* (New York: Basic Books, 2016).

5   Patrick Lencioni, *The Advantage: Why Organizational Health Trumps Everything Else in Business* (San Francisco: Jossey-Bass, 2012), 15–16.

aligns its resources to best achieve its goals, it is healthy and has the best chance of success.

For The United Methodist Church, the question of clarity focuses on the mission statement in paragraphs 120–122 of *The Book of Discipline*. These paragraphs were adopted in 1996 and have been slightly modified since that time. In those twenty-one years, we can point to one success and two failures as we have lived into the mission statement. The success is that the phrase "make disciples of Jesus Christ for the transformation of the world" is widely known and easily repeated.

The first failure is that there is a lack of understanding of what the mission statement means. We have not overcommunicated clarity. Paragraph 122 gives an outline of the holistic process with five key points:

- Proclaim the gospel.
- Lead persons to commit their lives to God through Christ.
- Nurture persons in Christian living.
- Send persons to live lovingly and justly in the world.
- Continue the mission of seeking, welcoming, and gathering.

The intent of the General Conference was not fulfilled. Sixteen years after the adoption of the mission statement, the Towers-Watson study of the denomination found that while many persons could repeat the short phrase "to make disciples of Jesus Christ for the transformation of the world," few could explain what it means. The five bulleted points summarized above have not penetrated the collective mind of the church.

The second failure is the all-too-frequent refusal to align our resources in light of the mission. Many persons felt that the Call to Action arising out of the 2009 financial crisis in the United States was an opportunity for shifting denominational priorities. The Council of Bishops and Connectional Table said: "Thus, the adaptive challenge for

The United Methodist Church is: To redirect the flow of attention, energy, and resources to an intense concentration on fostering and sustaining an increase in the number of **vital congregations** effective in making disciples of Jesus Christ for the transformation of the world."[6]

Most of the efforts at General Conference in 2012 seeking to implement these changes failed to pass or were declared unconstitutional by the Judicial Council. In response, some General Agencies and a few annual conferences have sought to realign priorities, but the changes have been minimal.

Further, efforts at responding in significant ways to the adaptive challenge have been derailed by the denomination's crisis over human sexuality. The attention of key leaders has been diverted to the Commission on a Way Forward in hopes that it will bring to the Council of Bishops a workable solution to our constitutional crisis. Not since 1844 have bishops and annual conferences engaged in principled disobedience to the order and discipline of the church. The uncertainty about the future of the connection paralyzes people who are no longer sure if they will be United Methodist in 2021.

> The UMC holds within its life and doctrine
> the seeds for a vibrant Wesleyan movement.

The main idea of this chapter is that the recent history of The UMC holds within its life and doctrine the seeds for a vibrant Wesleyan movement in the United States. Yet there will be difficult and significant changes required to become that kind of movement again. For each of the five cultural changes discussed above, The United Methodist Church has what it needs to meet its adaptive challenge.

---

6 See "A Call to Action for The United Methodist Church: Final Report of the Interim Operations Team, September 2012," located at www.umc.org/calltoaction. See Steering Team Report, p. 8 of 248.

Becoming a Movemental Institution

Many persons in the baby boom generation were trained to think of institutions as bad. Often people will contrast institutions with movements and say: "Methodism needs to become a movement again. We must not care about saving the institution." The deep irony of such statements is they are often made by pastors and bishops whose salaries, benefits, and ability to effect change all depend on their position within an institution. Institutions are crucial for impacting the world because of their resources, people, and traditions.

Instead, we need to work at becoming a movemental institution; that is, one where its purpose is at the center of all that it does. All too often institutions drift away and start investing their resources in too many disjointed efforts. That is certainly the case with The United Methodist Church in many of its components. We need to strip away the things that distract our time, people, and money away from our main mission.

One of the most important efforts is the discussion about a global book of Discipline. This is first and foremost an opportunity to strip away rules and requirements that, however well intentioned, prevent nimbleness and effectiveness at the level where mission is being accomplished. Too many United Methodist leaders have been trained to think that following the rules in the Discipline will accomplish their purpose. We need to retrain ourselves to focus on fruitful expressions of our purpose whether or not the minutiae of the Discipline are followed.

Similarly, we need to relearn how to distinguish excellence from mediocrity. Excellence in ministry furthers the church's purpose. Mediocrity settles for following the rules and procedures that are prescribed in the Discipline or have been inherited. It has frequently been said that the six last words of the church are "We've always done it that way." In a world that is changing rapidly, blind adherence to what worked in the 1950s or '60s is a recipe for failure.

In its heyday, Methodism was a movemental institution that was prepared to focus on its mission of reforming the nation and spreading scriptural holiness. It had a minimal set of rules and trusted its bishops and clergy to lead effectively in their local contexts. We are capable of becoming that kind of organization again. Becoming a movement is the way to adapt to today's world and get out of the 1950s.

Embodying a Way of Life

If the Enlightenment has captured the culture, it has also failed at creating a single way of life based on reason. Human beings have turned out to be less rational than philosophers expected, and the variety of ways of life has increased dramatically. This is especially seen in the debates about human sexuality, where the list of sexual orientations and gender identities keeps growing with significant implications for human rights and family structures. Religion has not faded away as some predicted. Instead, many different religious options now vie for places in the culture and recognition by societal institutions.

The future of Christianity in such a diverse world is similar to its situation during the Roman Empire, where a variety of religions competed in a diverse political unit. Loren Mead saw this thirty years ago in his book *The Once and Future Church*. Methodism will thrive in the future not as the established church supported by the culture but as a community of love and high moral standards, which give people support in a way of life that will be attractive to those turned off by the other alternatives in the culture.

This approach requires clarity and consistency of our message. United Methodism's official doctrine lies clearly within the mainstream of Christian orthodoxy. We share with other Christians the faith expressed in the Apostles' and Nicene Creeds. In addition, we tend to minimize controversies over nonessential teachings, such as modes of baptism and expectations of the end times. We do focus on the way of salvation and the means of grace. And we care deeply about sanctification as the pursuit of personal and social holiness.

Many of the criticisms of Christianity expressed by non-Christian persons do not apply to United Methodist doctrine as officially expressed. We believe in the authority of scripture as interpreted by tradition, reason, and experience and thereby avoid criticisms of Christians as unthinking and ignorant of modern science. We believe in sharing faith verbally, thereby creating a worldview that emphasizes a loving God transforming the world. At the same time we teach that our faith must be put into action and make a difference in combatting social sins such as poverty, racism, and sexism. We teach the universal love of God that embraces all people. We also acknowledge that salvation is a present reality as well as quality of life after death. Thus, we can talk with nonbelievers about how to find meaning and purpose here on earth.

Such a way of life, when presented in contextually appropriate ways, can be a compelling alternative to the hedonistic and nihilistic approaches that also vie for the loyalty of people today. We are not in a situation where any one ideology or approach is going to be seen as universally obvious to all. Indeed, the criteria for judging acceptability is even in dispute. Instead, the compelling attractiveness of Christian love will once again bring people to faith, just as it did in the first three centuries of Christianity's rise. The words of Aristides's apology to the Emperor Hadrian remind us of how we attracted people in those times:

> They love one another. They never fail to help widows. They save orphans from those who would hurt them. If they have something, they give freely to the man who has nothing. If they see a stranger, they take him home and are happy, as though he were a real brother. They don't consider themselves brothers in the usual sense, but brothers instead through the Spirit, in God.[7]

---

7 Aristides, "The Apology of Aristides the Philosopher," *Early Christian Writings*, trans. D.M. Kay, accessed October 2, 2016, http://www.earlychristianwritings.com/text/aristides-kay .html.

Teaching and preaching the Wesleyan way of salvation is the antidote to the Enlightenment's cultural victory.

Creating Community

In a public lecture in Lawrence, Kansas, Robert Putnam was describing the collapse of community and how it might be remedied. To a secular university audience he said, "God, we need more preachers." After pausing, he added, "I said that right." He then went on to describe how preachers have in the past done a great job of creating social capital by gathering persons into communities based on a common faith.

During its first 150 years in England and America, Methodism put a high priority on the formation of small groups. Participation in first the class meeting and then the Sunday school was a requirement in the Wesleyan way of salvation. During the last fifty years, various attempts at recreating a small-group experience have been made with varying degrees of success. Some of the largest and most fruitful congregations in the United States have established small accountability groups and communicated a high expectation of participation for their members.

The renewal of the small-group approach to discipleship is a key ingredient for the kind of fruitful, movemental Methodism that I envision. We know how to do this, and we have the resources to make it happen. What we need is the commitment of leaders in conferences and local congregations to bring it about. Creating community is the antidote to Americans' pervasive loneliness.

Living Inclusiveness

When The United Methodist Church was formed in 1968, it committed itself to ending segregation and fostering inclusiveness. For the last fifty years there has been a focus on making all connectional committees and the episcopacy inclusive with regard to race and gender.

We have committed ourselves to open itinerancy so that clergy are appointed without regard to race and gender. We have also made some attempts at creating multicultural congregations where at least 20 percent of the worshipping congregation is from a different ethnic group than the majority.

There is often a lively debate about how well we have lived out our commitment to inclusiveness. By any measure, we have made progress at including persons of color and women in the Council of Bishops, General Conference delegations, and staff of general agencies. At the same time, we have seen a great weakening of African American lay membership, and we still do not have many women appointed as senior pastors of large congregations. We lag far behind in reaching Hispanics. The percentage of the Hispanic population is almost always higher than the percentage of their membership in The United Methodist Church.

My point here is that the struggles for inclusiveness have given us resources for the future. We have had experience with diverse leadership, and that experience will help us missionally in an increasingly diverse America. Having women as clergy and including women as bishops is an advantage in American culture. Having persons of color as pastors is crucial to reaching communities of color with the gospel.

Once again there is an advantage in our doctrinal perspective of universal redemption and our strong witness against racism and sexism. It is in developing better cultural intelligence and looking for opportunities to enhance the leadership of women and persons of color that will enable significant progress in the future. Leveraging our experience of inclusiveness is the best response to the significant increase in the diversity of the American people.

Branding Our Connection

Digital communication has enhanced a long-term trend toward national brands. Advertising on network television, cable television, the

Internet, as well as in print media all create a nationwide identity for various groups. One can think of slogans such as "Just do it" and visual symbols such as Nike's swoosh that communicate widely to many different audiences. Statistics vary about how much time people spend online and in front of a television, but in the last fifty years we have seen a significant increase in how people are digitally influenced. Apps on smartphones may be just the latest way in which organizations try to influence people to buy, watch, or join.

The United Methodist Church was late to adapt to this new communications environment. We were successful in the days of print media. In the first half of the nineteenth century, we had one of the largest communication networks in America using books and newspapers to reach people. As radio became more important, followed by television and then the Internet, we were slow to recognize the opportunities that digital communication offered. An important step was taken with the Igniting Ministries campaign and the adoption of the "Open Hearts. Open Minds. Open Doors" campaign in 2000.

Once again, there is lively debate about how well we did with this branding. The slogan was chosen because professional market research concluded that unchurched people were most attracted to the openness of United Methodist theology and congregations. The very existence of the phrase led many to use it in local advertising. From that point of view it was successful. Yet many offered strong criticisms. Progressives noted that United Methodist rules were not fully open to the inclusion of lesbian, gay, bisexual, transgendered, and queer persons, and thus the slogan was a form of false advertising. Conservatives noted that the slogan made no mention of God, Jesus, or faith and portrayed United Methodism as a wishy washy "believe anything" group.

Nevertheless, the campaign was an important step in embracing digital communication and experimenting with the kind of message such media require. In digital culture there is still a role for printed articles, papers, and books. But increasingly people will not pay attention to such media unless they are first introduced to a short visually compelling form of the message. We have made such changes in our communications technology in the past, and we have been experimenting with them recently. Local churches are improving their websites, and conferences are investing more money in communications staff and budgets. The proliferation of forms of social media has made communication strategies both more complicated and more expensive and there is much improvement that needs to be made.

The most difficult issue for branding is the decision about what The United Methodist Church stands for and how to make sure that our brand is actually embodied in local churches. Part of the success behind the modern franchise model is that a national communications strategy actually describes what one can find at the local franchise. The theological diversity of The United Methodist Church, combined with the unfruitfulness and stagnation of many congregations, makes a communications strategy hard to design. For example, there is a standardization in all McDonald's franchises so that a customer knows what to expect when walking into the restaurant. Walking into a conservative UMC congregation in Texas is a different experience than worshipping in a reconciling UMC congregation in California. Even within the same city there are churches with extremely different worship styles, making communicating what it means to be a United Methodist Christian a difficult task. Improving our message and enhancing our digital presence in the culture is the right response to a flat world.

Becoming a Movement Again

This vision of a vital, movemental United Methodist Church is worth pursuing. Counting the time I chaired committees of the North Texas Annual Conference and then served on the faculty of Perkins School of Theology, I have invested more than twenty-five years in connectional ministry seeking to help the Church move in this direction. Based on my experience as an elected conference leader, seminary professor, and bishop, I have come to three conclusions about how we can best move forward in this direction.

First, the most important place where vital ministry happens is in the local church. The 1996 General Conference expressed this in the second sentence of the mission statement, "Local churches provide the most significant arena through which disciple-making occurs." It was also expressed in the Call to Action's focus on increasing the number of vital congregations. The most recent General Conference added the words "and extension ministries of the Church" to the sentence. This was a frequently experienced dilution of our focus in order to be inclusive of places and people within our connection. In my view, extension ministries exist to strengthen local churches. Our camps play a crucial role in forming children, youth, and adults for the purpose of improving their discipleship back home. Our campus ministries reach people during a formative period in their lives. Hospital chaplains are ministering to people during seasons of illness. All of these ministries are important, but they still point back to the importance of disciple-making in the local church.

This focus on the local congregation is deeply tied to what it means to be a disciple of Jesus. Discipleship means disciplined participation in the means of grace that constitute the life and ministry of local congregations. Weekly worship, frequent communion, weekly small group meetings, and sacrificial service to the poor all happen best in the local church. All of those activities also happen in connectional gatherings and extension ministries, but they are all aimed at deepening the kind of discipleship that is lived out only in local churches.

A crucial corollary of this claim is that more resources should be poured into local churches. This means reducing the apportionments paid by local congregations so they have more money to fund disciple-making ministries. It also means that annual conferences and general agencies should have in the forefront of their planning and priorities steps to strengthen local congregations.

Second, the three most important factors in the vitality of congregations are leadership, leadership, and leadership. While lay leadership is important, the systemic key to renewing the church is for the connection to provide excellent clergy leadership. When we think about what helps United Methodism be its best, the key element is our leadership development and deployment system. Our ability to credential persons and then make them available for appointment gives us a reliable supply of preachers. In my thirteen years as bishop, the single most important factor in the revitalization of congregations is the leadership of the pastor.

Third, we need to make progress in the following six areas of that system: spiritual revival, recruitment, education, credentialing, appointing, and exiting.

Spiritual Revival

There is a low level of spiritual power among many United Methodist clergy. Most function in pastoral ways to maintain the church rather than sensing any urgency about making disciples and transforming the world. The occasional exceptions have shown us what holistic Wesleyan evangelism and social action can do.

Attention needs to be paid to improving ways of nurturing a spiritual revival among United Methodist clergy. In my own experience Disciple Bible Study and the Walk to Emmaus were formative. Experiences I had in those two places both lit spiritual fires within me and sustained those fires throughout my pastoral ministry. We ought to be seeking out ways of fostering similar experiences for the next generation of leaders.

Recruitment

The oft-repeated mantra (coined by Lovett Weems) "more people, more young people, and more diverse people" indicates that we should recruit more clergy, more young clergy, and more diverse clergy. This generation of young persons is different from my generation, and recruiting them in large numbers means that annual conferences must become much more intentional about their efforts.

The Texas Annual Conference has six steps in place to address this issue:

- Our camp at Lakeview Conference Center places an emphasis on inviting high school–age persons to make commitments for full-time Christian service. Camp staff then track those young persons and coordinate with local churches, seminaries, and campus ministries to help nurture that call.

- Each summer we hold the Texas Youth Academy as an advanced discipleship program for senior high youth. It offers participants a two-week intensive educational experience of learning about the Christian faith and ministry.

- Our campus ministries at colleges within the bounds of the conference are important places where young persons hear about the possibility of God's call to full-time ministry.

- We offer a college pastoral intern program where college students can be interns at selected local churches. It is intended for those interested in exploring ministry as a career.

- We offer Ambassador's Grants to help pay for debt related to tuition and fees accumulated in seminary. Each clergy can receive up to $25,000 over five years.

- We offer Advancing Pastoral Leadership and Transforming Pastoral Leadership groups to enhance the leadership skills of persons who have been ordained. These cohorts offer participants important peer-learning experiences with a facilitator to help them develop their leadership skills.

To fund these programs the conference is raising $12 million for its Emerging Leaders Endowment. The goal is to create a well-funded, sustainable ecology of call that will ensure the best possible young leadership for the future of the Wesleyan movement in our conference.

Education

There was a time when a network of United Methodist colleges and universities actually formed students in Wesleyan Christianity. With only a few exceptions that network has disappeared. Schools nominally related to The UMC are often secular and have little formative power for raising up United Methodist leaders. At the same time our official United Methodist seminaries have more loyalty to the academy than to the doctrine and polity of the church. Academic excellence is most often construed in ways that cultivate hostility to the official teachings of The UMC. Our current relationships to seminaries presume that excellence in academic work will contribute positively to excellence in church leadership. The relationship between what the academy regards as excellent and what serves the church's mission is no longer an automatic connection. We dare not assume it exists.

 Knowledge and vital piety should
be strongly joined together.

I write as one who firmly believes that knowledge and vital piety should be strongly joined together. However, the institutional loyalties developed since 1945 have militated against the vitality of the church. Where strong deans and presidents have led theological schools to hold both the academy and the church as equally important judges of excellence, theological education has served the church's mission well. This task has been made more difficult by the dilution of the Church's voice. No effective body of the denomination represents the Church's needs to theological schools. Occasional attempts are made, but the respect for academic freedom and the deference paid to the academy has always weakened the ability of the church to first decide on what it wants and then to articulate it with authority. The University Senate and its Commission on Theological Education need to be reconfigured to speak more clearly for the needs of the church's mission.

Credentialing

Boards of Ordained Ministry need to be redesigned to work in close collaboration with bishops and cabinets. They should be credentialing the kinds of clergy who will lead the church toward greater vitality. All too often they choose to follow the requirements in *The Book of Discipline* as if they were a checklist to be mechanically followed. Instead, careful personnel judgments need to be made along the lines of, "Would this person, if appointed as senior pastor, grow one of the churches of our conference?" There are too many rules and not enough good judgment shaping the work of boards.

Bishops and cabinets have often been less than exemplary in the credentialing process. Far too often we have sought to be nice and to avoid the difficult conversations of telling persons the truth about their performance. Boards that function well rely on input from those who directly experience the candidate's ministry, and our culture of "niceness" often credentials persons who do not belong in ordained ministry.

In some conferences a history of antagonism between cabinets and the board has made good decision-making difficult to achieve. At their worst boards functioned as union stewards to protect clergy from any negative consequences. At their worst bishops and cabinets have acted arbitrarily and unfairly without due process and clear communication. In a vibrant Wesleyan movement all parts of the credentialing process will be focused on raising up clergy leaders who can effectively make disciples of Jesus Christ for the transformation of the world.

Appointing

The drift of United Methodism since 1968 can be traced to two chief causes. First, we deliberately weakened the office of bishop by restricting episcopal authority. Second, we enhanced benefits and protection for clergy careers. This eroded the appointive process so that clergy came to expect an increase in salary and size of church every time they moved. Appointments came to be based on seniority and career rather than on the needs of the local church.

A number of bishops have been working hard to make appointments based on the missional effectiveness of local churches. This has led to younger persons being appointed ahead of older persons who believed they were next in line for a particularly desirable appointment. It has also led to the increased use of numerical measures of effectiveness as cabinets and bishops sought to make good judgments about an individual's capabilities to grow churches.

The other factor here is affinity. Bishops and cabinets have learned that cultural affinities are often crucial determinants of a person's success. Such affinities can include ethnicity, geography, gender, and theological convictions. If there was ever a time when any given Methodist clergy could effectively serve any given Methodist congregation, those days are long gone. We do value open itinerancy for women and persons of color, but such appointments require a high degree of cultural intelligence in order to be successful. To have a vibrant Wesleyan movement requires movemental bishops who make good personnel judgments and have the freedom and resources to act boldly. When such freedom exists, bishops must have the backbone to act wisely for the purposes of the church.

Exiting

Two factors raise to a high level the importance of exiting persons from ordained ministry. First, the nature of religion in American culture is vastly different than it used to be. Some persons who entered ministry thirty years ago had a vision of what church leadership involved based on what it had been prior to that time. The changing realities of the church mean that the sense of calling they had back then is no longer effective in the early twenty-first century. They have not achieved the kind of success they anticipated, and they would be happier and more fulfilled doing something else. They might even be better disciples as laypeople than as clergy in the current environment. Yet, for family and financial reasons, leaving ordained ministry is difficult. The Voluntary Transition Program of Wespath is an important vehicle for addressing such situations.

The second factor is that the missional drift of United Methodism and its leadership development system allowed a number of persons into full connection who should never have been ordained at all. We have made too many poor personnel decisions and thus made lifetime promises to persons. When they lead local churches into decline, they rightfully expect the promise of an appointment to be kept. When Boards of Ordained Ministry function as protectors of clergy benefits rather than agents of church vitality, such persons are kept in conference membership far too long.

Paragraph 359 of *The Book of Discipline 2016* offers a workable pathway for administrative location on the basis of ineffectiveness. I fully support giving clergy clear evaluations and naming the behaviors that cause it. However, the process has to be used rigorously and in a timely manner by bishops and in cooperation with their boards of ordained ministry.

Conclusion

I believe that a vibrant Wesleyan movement is possible to achieve in the next twenty years. Some unnamed person once summarized its possibility in a brief and overstated summary: "If a great revival ever comes to America, it will come through the Wesleyans. They have done it before if they will only remember it. They have the right doctrine if they will only preach it. They have the right organization if they will only use it." May it be so.

In a radically changing world, the Wesleyan movement in general and The United Methodist Church in particular have exactly what

Americans need to thrive. The cultural realities of American life present historic challenges and opportunities for the Wesleyan movement. Whether The United Methodist Church seizes its opportunity will determine how fruitfully this part of the Wesleyan movement defines itself and adapts to its new mission context.

Questions for Discussion

1. How is your church and ministry different today than it was twenty years ago? When was the heyday of your church?

2. Briefly share your thoughts about the vitality of your church. How is your church growing? On a scale of one to ten (one being low and ten being high), how would you rate the vitality of your church? Your district? Your conference? The denomination? How can you help?

3. How would a visibly vital denomination make your ministry more effective?

4. Do you agree that disciple-making happens best in the local church? Why or why not?

5. What seemingly insurmountable obstacles and challenges are you experiencing in your church? Make a list. Then on this list, note how each obstacle might become an opportunity.

6. In order to be more responsive to people in need, what would you change in the church? In the Discipline?

7. State the central message of your church in one short sentence. Is it possible for The United Methodist Church as a denomination to have a single, clear message? What would it be?

8. Loneliness is still a primary affliction for people of all ages. How does your church create and nurture community?

9. How does your church live out inclusivity?

10. Do you feel heard by your district superintendent and/or bishop? How might they serve you better?

11. What do you know about the work of the general church agencies? How might they better communicate with local churches?

12. How does your church use digital media to communicate its message? Is this now or should this be a priority?

13. Discuss leadership in your local situation. What are ten things that a good leader does? What are ten things a leading church does? Make a list.

14. Balancing the personal needs of clergy to make a viable living with the needs of the church can be difficult. How can The UMC better recruit, equip, and support clergy? What is the role of the local church, the district superintendent, the Board of Ministry, and the bishop?

15. How hopeful are you about the future of the church? If your church closed its doors tomorrow, who would notice?

16. If you knew you could not fail and had all power of heaven on your side, how would you engage for a vibrant Wesleyan movement?

Engage
for Such a Time as This

J. Michael Lowry

Resident Bishop of the Fort Worth Episcopal
Area, The United Methodist Church

Religions die. Over the course of history, some religions vanish altogether, while others are reduced from great world faiths to a handful of adherents . . .

It is not difficult to find countries or even continents, once viewed as natural homelands of a particular faith, where that creed is now extinct, and such disasters are not confined to primal or "primitive" beliefs. The systems that we think of as great world religions are as vulnerable to destruction as was the faith of the Aztecs or Mayans in their particular gods.

Christianity, too, has on several occasions been destroyed in regions where it once flourished. In most cases, the elimination has been so thorough as to obliterate any memory that Christians were ever there, so that today any Christian presence whatsoever in these parts is regarded as a kind of invasive species derived from the West.[1]

---

1 Philip Jenkins, *The Lost History of Christianity: The Thousand-Year Golden Age of the Church in the Middle East, Africa, and Asia—and How It Died* (New York: HarperCollins, 2008), 1–2.

Facing Our Demise

"Religions die." The stark words with which Philip Jenkins opens his book *The Lost History of Christianity: The Thousand-Year Golden Age of the Church in the Middle East, Africa, and Asia— and How It Died* offer a sobering reminder of the larger issues at stake behind the current struggle of The United Methodist Church (especially in its American branch) to fully embrace our missio Dei, God's mission for the Church. While the temptation of peremptory arrogance suggests an easy dismissal of such a large claim, a narrower focus on the Wesleyan witness of the Christian faith ought rightly to give us pause. A glance eastward to Northern Europe, where the Christian faith once held dominance, forms a shadow over the backdrop of our current missional groupings.

In a more focused American setting, Jim Collins's *How the Mighty Fall: And Why Some Companies Never Give In* chronicles the decline and eventual failure of corporations that once towered over the landscape of corporate America. In reading his book I could not help but think that I was reading the story of The United Methodist Church in the latter part of the twentieth century and the first two decades of the twenty-first century. At one time, The United Methodist Church (through its various predecessors) could claim an adherence of roughly 34 percent of the population in the United States. Today our national market share is closer to 1 percent. (In the Central Texas Conference our market share is 1.1 percent of the population. The Central Texas Conference occupies the medium for the South Central Jurisdiction.) The first chapter of *How the Mighty Fall,* as laid out by Collins's work, speaks volumes to our easy assumption of invulnerability—"Hubris Born of Success." While such business language tends to offend some United Methodist pastors and academicians, reality is what it is. Long gone is the day when the missional strength of The United Methodist Church (and more so, even the need for church at all) can be culturally assumed. Put bluntly, we are a dying institution existing in a culture where the very assumptions of the Christian faith and the need for the church are up for grabs.

There is still much vitality left in The United Methodist Church.

To be sure, it must be noted that our current deceptive strength would offer a reason to dismiss such a grim prognosis. Furthermore, the march of time is slow and, at our present rate of decline, one could argue that The United Methodist Church has years of life left in it and that any prognosis of imminent death is quite premature. Nonetheless, The United Methodist Church *as we know it* (the phrase "as we know it" is a towering qualifier) is slowly collapsing around us. This slow-motion collapse may take a long time to play out, and then again it may hit a tipping point and cascade rapidly downward. Either way, it will be painful, causing heartache and much anxiety.

Yet careful reflection merits a studied pause in my narrative. There is still much vitality left in The United Methodist Church. Creative responses to the pounding waves of an increasing secularity abound. A reasonable person might note:

- the Fresh Expressions movement;
- new Faith Communities;
- rising engagement in outreach; missional activities for the hungry, hurting, and homeless;
- reawakening small-group gatherings for spiritual formation; and
- the evident hunger all along the theological spectrum for authentic spiritual encounters with God.

Taken together (and this is surely only a partial listing) these fresh signs of health and vitality point to a future of hope. There can be little doubt that the Holy Spirit is moving among us in The United Methodist Church of our day and time. Philip Jenkins offers his own counterweight to the opening lines of *The Lost History of Christianity* near the end of the book when he writes:

Responding to a threat of persecution, sixteenth-century Protestant Theodore Beza urged a foe to "remember that the
Church is an anvil that has worn out many a hammer." The history of all the great world faiths proves that religions are highly
resilient, and difficult to eradicate. History is littered with false
claims about the imminent deaths of religions, claims that in
retrospect make almost comic reading. The first known contemporary reference to the Jewish people is an Egyptian inscrip-
tion boasting that "Israel is laid waste: his seed is no more."
Mark Twain remarked on how often the world had turned out
for the burial of Roman Catholicism, only to find it postponed
yet again, "on account of the weather or something. . . . Ap-
parently one of the most uncertain things in the world is the
funeral of a religion."

Faiths are dynamic, and periods of difficulty or persecution can have the effect of forcing believers to delve into the
rich diversity of traditions that have evolved over thousands of
years. Usually, they find at least some ideas and practices that
proved effective in adapting to the new world, and that can in
fact provide the foundation for significant revival.[2]

It should be noted that, ironically, such a qualifier comes at the beginning of a chapter entitled "How Faiths Die."

With both a grim glimpse at the possible death of a vibrant Methodist expression of faith (at least on any large scale) and a caution-
ary note that "history is littered with false claims about the imminent
deaths of religions,"[3] the struggle over a recovery of Methodism as
a missional movement for the Lord looms large before us. We must
confess that "we see in a mirror, dimly" (1 Cor. 13:12, NRSV). In this
chapter, I argue that the heart of our crisis is theological. We need
a recovery of deep orthodoxy if The United Methodist Church is to
have a future.

---

2   Jenkins, *The Lost History of Christianity*, 207–8.

3   Jenkins, *The Lost History of Christianity*, 207.

Concomitant with such a recovery of deep orthodoxy, the missio Dei of The United Methodist Church must recover the will and way of a vibrant evangelistic witness that is unafraid to lift up Jesus as the Christ and call for conversion and transformation in radical allegiance to Christ as Lord and Savior. To this end, I will offer (with the assistance of Rev. Lance Marshall, pastor of The Gathering) a new faith community emerging out of First United Methodist Church in Fort Worth, Texas, as one example of just how a revived theological orthodoxy combined with evangelistic witness and missional praxis might look.

The Great Need for an Orthodox Recovery

With this duel of demise and hesitantly emerging new life as a backdrop held in tension, imagine for a moment that the major issues that threaten The United Methodist Church with schism were somehow resolved to everyone's satisfaction—LGBTQI/human sexuality, abortion, racism, economic injustice, war, and so forth. Such a dreamed-of, peaceable kingdom in The United Methodist Church would not by itself launch us into a renewed period of movemental growth, however one defines such faithfulness and fruitfulness (i.e., numerical, spiritual, missional, or some combination). The malaise that grips us is deeper than any one social or ethical issue.

There is a growing sense among some bishops that we work side by side with two kinds of churches. One kind of church is the fading, declining old mainline with its renewed emphasis on missional outreach largely divorced from an explicit gospel witness (which often comes across as an advanced version of moralistic therapeutic deism). The other kind is an orthodox, vibrant expression of the church, which can't help but reach across ethnic and class lines. By its very nature such a church, grounded in the gospel, instinctively understands that doctrine and practice cannot be separated. Furthermore, the emerging church is passionately, outwardly focused in a way that is evangelistically as well as missionally engaged with the growing non-Christian environment.

The search and experimentation for "something more" being conducted on the edge of Methodism offers a further hint both at the hunger for substance and the slowly awakening conviction that the theology we largely have been pursuing for the past half century or more is largely bankrupt. Our hyper-reaction against evangelical fundamentalism (a mistake of the first order—evangelicalism and fundamentalism are not the same!) and an uncritical embrace of enlightenment, intellectual biases have led us into the cul-de-sac of a vague therapeutic moral deism (to use the term popularized by Dr. Kenda Creasy Dean in her book *Almost Christian: What the Faith of Our Teenagers Is Telling the American Church*). We are increasingly aware that attempts to split doctrine and practice (or orthodoxy and orthopraxy) are inherently destructive. When orthopraxy is split off from a deep connection to orthodoxy, the Christian faith is cut off from its life-giving roots. The resultant expression of Christianity is inherently emaciated and entering a death spiral.[4]

The gnawing spiritual hunger that surrounds us (even engulfs us) is finding its thirst quenched at the fount of orthodox theology, especially orthodox Wesleyan theology. One of my new district superintendents (himself on the progressive side of the LGBTQI/human sexuality divide) commented on visiting the churches of his district:

> When I walk into a worship service at one of our churches, it only takes a few minutes to sense a fundamental difference between churches that are alive and vibrant and those that feel empty and hollow. Most of us would point to the normal

---

4 "What is clear is that genuine Christianity, wherever it expresses itself, is always in tension with significant aspects of the surrounding culture, because it always seeks to transform it. Movements are transformative by name, so they do not accept the status quo. On the other hand, theologically liberal Christianity, while sincere, seeks to minimize this tension—that is why liberalism is often called cultural Christianity. And that is why it is just about impossible to find a liberal movement that has made any significant missional impact on the world. Liberalism comes later in the life of a movement and usually is a clear signal of decline." (Alan Hirsch, *The Forgotten Ways: Reactivating the Missional Church* [Grand Rapids, MI: Brazos Press, 2006], 191.)

difference makers like radical hospitality, committed missional work, excellence in music, gifted preachers, strong lay leadership, etc. But the obvious difference I see is between those that have a high Christology and those that don't. It's not about size, location, money, or resources. It doesn't matter if the church is big, small, rural, urban, traditional, or progressive. If Christ is at the center of the church, it changes everything. The churches who lift up Christ appear to have a clearer vision, a deeper mission, and a burning passion to offer Christ to the world. If Christ isn't at the center of the church, it can feel like a well-intentioned, therapeutic self-help program that provides good advice for the living but cannot offer salvation to those who are lost.[5]

 The gnawing spiritual thirst that engulfs us can be quenched at the fount of orthodox Wesleyan theology.

Alongside such observations, the fashionable Protestant progressivism of American high culture increasingly looks like an emperor with no clothes. A prominent lay leader and newly retired senior executive from a major corporation responds this way to the notion that Methodism is about believing in God and doing good without any specific need for Jesus other than by way of example and teaching: "If that's all there is, why bother?"

Rather than an excessive focus on gender preferences, I want to argue that we have been engaged as a denomination in extended affairs with various new versions of heresy: moralistic therapeutic deism; missional plagiarism; and political infatuations of both the right and the left, iced over with a prosperity gospel that surreptitiously tugs at

---

5   Rev. Ben Disney, East District superintendent, the Central Texas Conference. The East District includes some of the largest churches in United Methodism and is largely urban and suburban, though there are a significant number of rural and county seat congregations.

the heart of the crumbling mainline edifice. (With regard to the prosperity gospel, consider the casual embrace of financial resources and upper–middle class status that accompany the hidden assumptions of virtually all United Methodists, including myself.)

Alister McGrath rightly notes, "Heresy was a flawed, deficient, anemic, and inauthentic form of Christian faith that was inevitably doomed to extinction in the pluralist and intensely competitive world of late classical antiquity." And, we should carefully add, in the pluralistic and intensely competitive world of the early twenty-first century. He continues, "Orthodoxy had greater survival potential, prompting a 'search for authenticity' as a means of safeguarding its future."[6]

The new, or more accurately renewed, Church, which the Lord is calling into being out of the old "mainline" will be smaller, leaner, and more doctrinally coherent. We will recover, we are recovering, some sense of what it means to say Jesus is Lord and to assert core doctrines of incarnation, sin, justification, and sanctification (to mention a few). I have come slowly, painfully to believe that the Holy Spirit is moving us away from a "big tent" Methodism (and "big tent" Christianity), which enjoys periodic affairs with heretical suitors, into a new movement of faithfulness and fruitfulness in the name of our Lord.

The Challenge Before Us[7]

I wish to assert that the fundamental challenge before the church today does not rest on an ethical response to the so-called hot-button issues of our time but on a deeper theological foundation (or the lack thereof).

A personal story places the challenge before us in its wider context. The conversation took place on a casual vacation Saturday afternoon in

---

6   Alister McGrath, *Heresy: A History of Defending the Truth* (New York: HarperOne, 2009), 83–84.

7   Most of this part of this chapter comes from a book I am currently working on, tentatively entitled *The Challenge of Why*.

the San Francisco area. As we sat in the backyard with my brother and sister-in-law, my wife and I inquired about what local churches were nearby where we could worship God the next day. Scott and Sharon do not belong to any local church and give no evidence of deep religious convictions. With charity and without condemnation, they are not Christian. But Jolynn and I thought they knew the area, and so we inquired.

 People ask: "Why bother?"

The two of them fumbled around trying to think of the nearest United Methodist Church. After a while they decided there might be one on a certain street a couple of miles away. They weren't sure. So I checked online and found the worship times. We invited them to go with us. Scott's answer was an intriguing one. He said, "Why? Why bother?" He continued, "If I go, they're going to tell me to be a nice person, to help others, and out here [in San Francisco] they're going to advocate something that sort of looks like the liberal wing of the Democratic Party. Well, I think I am a nice person. [For the record, I agree. He's a good person and a moral man.] And I've tried being a liberal Democrat. I don't think it works. I've tried being a conservative Republican. I don't think that much works either." He paused to reflect, adding something like this: "I appreciate the invitation, but why would we want to bother going to church? Even more, why would we want to bother being Christian?"

Why bother, indeed? There is more to this personal story, but it is my brother's haunting final questions that grip my mind. "Why would we want to bother going to church? Even more, why would we want to bother being Christian?" They are before us in stark terms. Many, indeed millions, intuitively and readily grasp the need for a spiritual and moral dimension to their lives. Dwight Eisenhower's assertion resonates across cultural lines today more so than when he first uttered the words: "Our form of government makes no sense unless it is founded in a deeply felt religious belief, and I don't care what it is."[8] Spirituality is not debated. The challenge is, what kind of spirituality? What kind of spiritual convictions, dare we say faith, should we hold? Even more concretely, the challenge before Christians must be faced without flinching. *Why bother being Christian?*

This is not a new question. What is new is the way "church" is divorced from religious experience, coherent theological reflection and the intensity with which Christians are being challenged by this question. Another version of the challenge of "why bother?" came from a lay leader in my conference. He challenged a group of clergy who focused the gospel narrowly on various deeds of service and acts of social justice. His challenge was phrased this way: "Why can't I just volunteer and work on a Habitat house? Why do I need to be part of the church?" The lay leader came to visit with me, profoundly disturbed by the weakness of the answers he received. He asked, "Why not just skip the middle man and leave it to God and be engaged in some good works?"

What should disturb us greatly is how poorly we are equipped to face the challenge of why. Hints of H. Richard Niebuhr's probing critique of cultural Christianity traverse the contours of my reflections. "A God without wrath brought men without sin into a Kingdom without judgment through the ministrations of a Christ without a Cross."[9] It is worth pausing to note carefully that the challenge that originates in the question "Why bother to be a part of a church or worship?" quickly connects to the deeper challenge "Why bother to be a Christian at all?" The heart of the issue is profoundly theological and deeply biblical.

It has been said that the evangelical or conservative wing of the Christian movement in America is the Republican Party at prayer, to

---

8   President Dwight David Eisenhower, taken from "God in the White House," *God in America*, accessed March 22, 2018, www.pbs.org/godinamerica/god-in-the-white-house/.

9   H. Richard Niebuhr, *The Kingdom of God in America* (New York: Harper & Brothers, 1959), 193.

which one can easily add that the liberal or progressive wing of the Christian movement in America is the Democratic Party gathered around a Habitat house. Despite the obvious distortion of the Christian movement across the American spectrum, both tongue-in-cheek statements carry a painful grain of truth. Furthermore, despite the presence of a rich biblical and theological tradition, the very catch-phrase "spiritual but not religious" betrays the need for a clear and convincing answer to the challenge of why.

A common answer to the "why bother?" question has taken cultural root in the North American mission field through a heartfelt appeal to moral rectitude and social justice. The driving theological conviction is built on the great commandment to love God and love others. From such a strong harbor, the Christian faith sets sail in holy crusade to improve human society. For many, this noble vision of the Christian faith gains its impetus from attempts to eradicate the blights of war, racism, sexism, hunger, and injustice in all their variety and form. The goal and the end of living is the transformation of society with some vague utopian notion of what a just society looks like.

However well intended, the competing options demonstrate the failure of an exclusively moralistic position at the heart of the church. The impetus is good, even holy, yet by themselves the claims reduce the Christian faith to the Pelagian notion of saving yourself through moral effort. What need is there of Christ and the church? Perceptively, Phyllis Tickle comments, "If on a Sabbath morning at 11:00 a.m.—and only at 11:00 a.m.—one can either build a Habitat for Humanity [house] or go to the mass, the Social Justice Christian will say that faith without works is meaningless and go build the house, albeit with some regret."[10] In time, if not nurtured by the deep roots of faith, the moralistic or social justice perspective withers like a tree without water. It is but a short

---

10 Phyllis Tickle, *The Great Emergence: How Christianity Is Changing and Why* (Grand Rapids, MI: Baker Books, 2008), 129.

step to drop the label "Christian" and engage from a singularly social justice perspective. It is worth further noting that study after study of behavior and attitudes among Americans point to little difference between those who profess faith in Christ and those who do not, between those who are church attenders and those who are not.[11]

Our son, now thirty-eight, has received degrees in both engineering and philosophy. As he has moved about the United States, he has stayed active in local churches, serving in various leadership roles. Through his moves he has had the opportunity to visit quite a number of churches. His insights are anecdotally telling. Nathan commented to me in frustration, "Dad, the typical Methodist sermon consists of three points. One, God loves you. Two, love each other. Three, come on you all, try harder to love each other!" His take on such incipient (and common!) Pelagianism offers scant incentive to those struggling with a "why bother?" mentality. The religious "nones" (those not belonging to and/or not practicing any formal religion) can get their fill of activities of love, justice, and mercy in a variety of other ways than through the church.

Stirred, not shaken (to borrow from James Bond), such an understanding of Christianity hardly merits getting out of bed on a Sunday morning. Yet the deep hunger to somehow be "spiritual" remains. What is lacking is a sense of compelling substance and experience of the divine. Our deep challenge remains the lack of theological and doctrinal core. This is all the more surprising given the stated theological core of The United Methodist Church in the Doctrinal Standards and Articles of Religion.[12]

The drive for a moralistic core often has been yoked with a thera-

---

11 A recent Gallup poll notes that many believe society would be better off if more people were religious, but there is no evidence of concomitant commitment to go with such data "Most Americans Say Religion Is Losing Influence in U.S.," *Gallup*, May 29, 2013, http://news.gallup.com/poll/162803/americans-say-religion-losing-influence.aspx. *Research by the Barna Group and the Pew Report on Religion in America share similar data.*

12 *The Book of Discipline of The United Methodist Church 2016*, Paragraphs 102–4, pp. 47–91.

peutic milieu. Evidence rises out of the sense of being nice, which permeates the casual cultural understanding of the Christian faith. This is well documented in the National Study of Youth and Religion (NSYR). Kenda Creasy Dean notes in reflection, "The other 60%— the majority of American teenagers, who disproportionately call themselves mainline Protestant or Roman Catholic—harbor an attitude toward religion that one researcher described as 'benign positive regard.'"[13]

The facile limpness of such a weak assertion points to the lack of theological depth not just in our youth but also in the wider mainline Protestant and Catholic culture. Dean goes on to comment, "While most teenagers agree that religion is good, even important (even if it is not particularly important to them), they cannot explain how or why this is so, and many of them believe religion makes no difference to them personally."[14]

Such theological confusion exemplified in moralistic therapeutic deism is a far cry from the apostle Paul's self-introduction to the Romans: "From Paul, a slave of Christ Jesus, called to be an apostle and set apart for God's good news" (Rom. 1:1, CEB). It is a shocking, even offensive statement, let alone a purported introduction to Christians in the great capital city of the Roman Empire. Rightly we rebuke and despise slavery in every form . . . and yet Paul brags of being a slave.

The glory and honor for Paul come as they must come for us in the pointed last three words of the phrase—"of Christ Jesus." Christ is the anointed one from God, the divinely sovereign Lord and Master. The label "Christ" is linked, fused, with the personal human name, "Jesus." In that first line, Paul fuses together an understanding of the divine Savior who is a human man. What will emerge as orthodox Christology through a series of ecumenical councils culminating at Chalcedon is outlined in the opening line of this great letter. Slaves of the way of

---

13 Kenda Creasy Dean, *Almost Christian: What the Faith of Our Teenagers Is Telling the American Church* (Oxford: Oxford University Press, 2010), 27–28.

14 Dean, *Almost Christian*, 28.

salvation are slaves of the one who alone is fully human and fully divine—Christ Jesus.

Paul reaches for the close of this powerful opening verse with a ringing statement of purpose. All of this is about being "set apart for God's good news" (Rom. 1:1, CEB). It is about the good news that God in Christ through the power of the Holy Spirit has visited and redeemed planet Earth.

If we are to embrace the future, then reclaiming our biblical and Wesleyan theological heritage is a necessary and central action we must take. Place the witness from the book of The Acts of the Apostles alongside the tepid theological vagueness found in most United Methodist churches today. The difference is striking. The biblical record demands attention. The modern chapel begs indifference. Or examine Wesley sometime on his wintry blast against deism in all its forms. It is telling. Wesley's sermon "The Case of Reason Impartially Considered" (1781) cautions against both under- and over-valuing reason. He speaks of reason "assisted by the Holy Ghost." His notion of God is not abstract and removed but present and active.

Our answer to the "why bother?" question involves a reclaiming of theological and biblical fullness and faithfulness.[15] It calls us to embrace

---

15 In today's religious climate, orthodoxy is seen by some as simply the voting preference of the majority at ecumenical council. The argument runs along the lines of asserting that orthodoxy gained ascendancy through political and autocratically hierarchical impositions of ruling church authorities. Such a false notion crumples under the impact of careful historical study. When Origen offered his writings to the larger church as an initial outline of orthodoxy, the church itself was a small minority sect with little measurable enforcement power or political clout. Alister McGrath comments: "The writings of Origen can be considered an attempt to identify 'orthodoxy' as the most consistent rendering of Scripture, . . . Yet this process was fundamentally concerned with the crystallization of the perceptions within the church, not the imposition of some predetermined outcome" (McGrath, *Heresy*, 202). In the Arian controversy, political power in the person of the emperor supported Arius. "In the end, political influence proved inadequate to sustain a deficient vision of the Christian faith" (McGrath, *Heresy*, 205). The vision of an overweening papacy viciously suppressing dissent does not stand up to historical examination. Arguably, the See of Rome was fourth in the patriarchal line of power behind Antioch, Constantinople, and Alexandria (see chapter 3 of *The Jesus Wars* by Philip Jenkins). Far from simply being an opinion that

the past for the future. Grand theological themes of incarnation, sin, salvation, sanctification, and resurrection (to offer a partial list) are at the center of the much-needed embrace of our missio Dei among United Methodists in the United States.

Embracing Evangelism

Upon coming to the Fort Worth Episcopal Area in 2008, I would speak to various groups of clergy and laity about the end of Christendom and about our entering a post-Christian era. I talked about how we could no longer assume Christian history (however dim) or background knowledge. Christ must be presented anew.

The response is fascinating. Clergy by and large were either indifferent or impatient. They commonly asserted that they were aware we were in a post-Christian era. However, in their action and pastoral/missional activity I could find little evidence (with some notable exceptions) of their engaging in their mission field in a way consistent with a culture that did not know Christ.

The laity (again with some notable exceptions) were often surprised. I recall hearing a lay leader rise at a Texas Methodist Foundation board meeting and forcefully comment, "What is this? We haven't heard of this before."

Neither lay nor clergy had any real sense of how to combine evangelism with missional outreach. Most clergy had little, if any, knowledge of how to evangelistically engage a non- or nominal Christian. Most laity assumed that such engagement must happen through the institutional church and/or the pastor. Evangelism was not just a concept reserved for the (often hated) "fundamentalists" but also something of which the culture essentially took care.

---

gained more votes than other opinions, orthodoxy slowly emerged through the formation of Christian identity. Orthodox doctrine became (and is still) the way boundary lines of faith and practice are maintained.

It is common to find deep engagement in so-called mission activities—food pantries, backpack ministries, mission trips, mentoring, Imagine No Malaria, and the like. It is less common but still possible to find engagement in justice ministries. In the Fort Worth Episcopal Area, one such activity is engaging in a branch of JFON (Justice for Our Neighbors), a justice ministry working with immigrants and for the reform of immigration in the United States. What is (with rare exception) lacking is any connection of these "sanctifying" activities with a vibrant doctrine of justification through offering Christ. Our theological bankruptcy has led to a spiritual starvation as we attempt to go it our own way. In truth, as both the earliest disciples in the book of Acts and the original Methodists understood, evangelism is the offering of Christ.

It is important to understand at the outset that we cannot define the term *evangelism* out of existence. Nor can evangelism be adequately subsumed under "radical hospitality."[16] It quite literally means tactics for sharing the good news. Evangelism is thus yoked to a doctrine of salvation. The theological link runs from a doctrine of sin through a robust Christology to an understanding of the order of salvation in its constituent part to an unapologetically evangelistic outreach in and through the life of the community of faith. Albert Outler notes that in the early Methodist movement, Wesley's favorite text was 1 Corinthians 1:30:[17] "It is because of God that you are in Christ Jesus. He became wisdom from God for us. This means that he made us righteous and holy, and he delivered us" (CEB).

> The burden of his evangelical message was always the same; the references are almost monotonous. He [Wesley] speaks of "preaching Christ," of "offering Christ," "proclaiming Christ," "declaring Christ," and so forth. As always it was the gospel of

---

16 To be sure, we must perforce engage in radical hospitality, but evangelism is more than just hospitality, however radical or vital.

17 Albert C. Outler, *Theology in the Wesleyan Spirit* (Nashville: Discipleship Resources, 1975), 45.

salvation by grace through faith, justification and deliverance through God's grace in Christ.[18]

It is hard to overstate the evangelistic emphasis in the book of Acts. From Pentecost onward, the invitation is to put your whole trust in Christ, receive his grace, and move forward in newness of life under his lordship. As such, it is always far more than merely a verbal or intellectual assertion. Trust, or faith, has the deeper connotation of allegiance to Christ alone.[19] The intent of evangelism is embodying commitment to the Lord Jesus Christ over one's life. It is still difficult to surpass the 1919 Anglican Archbishop definition. **"To evangelize is to present Jesus Christ in the power of the Holy Spirit, that men [people] shall come to put their trust in God through him, to accept him as their Savior, and serve him as their king in the fellowship of his Church."**[20] Another readily popular (and accurate definition) comes from the insightful pen of D. T. Niles.

> EVANGELISM is witness. It is one beggar telling another beggar where to get food. The Christian does not offer out of his bounty. He has no bounty. He is simply guest at his Master's table and, as evangelist, he calls others too. The evangelistic relation is to be "alongside of" not "over-against." The Christian stands alongside the non-Christian and points to the Gospel, the holy action of God. It is not his knowledge of God that he shares, it is to God Himself that he points.[21]

The rubbed-raw wound of much of North American mainline Christianity is that, while we assert to a vague value of evangelism, both theology and practice betray our lack of both belief in and practice

---

18 Outler, *Theology in the Wesleyan Spirit*, 46.

19 Matthew Bates, *Salvation by Allegiance Alone: Rethinking Faith, Works, and the Gospel of Jesus the King* (Grand Rapids, MI: Baker Academic, 2017).

20 The Anglican Archbishops Committee of Enquiry into the Evangelistic Work of the Church, 1919.

21 Daniel Thomas Niles, *That They May Have Life* (New York: Harper & Brothers, 1951), 96.

of evangelism. One particular story from Martha Grace Reese captures the close connection between answering the why and embracing evangelism. She writes:

> The idea for the Mainline Evangelism Project can probably be dated to one conversation I had with some of my favorite people. I was leading a retreat for eight smart, loving pastors of growing mainline churches. Off the cuff, I asked, "Hey, what difference does it make in your **own** life that you are a Christian?"
>
> Silence. **Loud** silence stretched on. And on. I stared around the circle in disbelief. Finally one volunteered hesitantly, "Because it makes me a better person???" That question hadn't been intended as a pop final. I was not raised in the church, so I have a very clear sense of having made a choice to become a Christian that went against the culture in which I had always lived. I have a good sense of what it is like to be Christian and what it is like **not** to be Christian. Most Christians and most pastors grew up in the church. They did not change cultures to get there.[22]

The story is telling on a variety of levels. First, there is no sense of a theological rationale behind the invitation to be a Christian and a member of the body of Christ, the Church. Second, there is little sense of how one might go about evangelizing others. Dormant, but I submit potently present, is the deep conviction that mainliners do not wish to sound or act like fundamentalists or even those moderately evangelical. As one person put it to me, "I left the Baptist Church to get away from this."

The recovery of the evangelistic enterprise is foundational to the missio Dei of The United Methodist Church in North America. I have tried to demonstrate that at its heart this is a deeply theological problem. The second crucial step in recovering a missio Dei worth the

---

22 Martha Grace Reese, *Unbinding the Gospel* (Atlanta: Chalice Press, 2006), 14; emphasis in the original.

theological convictions at the heart of the Wesleyan Way is combining theology with practice. We must learn again how to engage in evangelism in a post-Christian culture.

At stake for the Methodist movement is reclaiming the past for the future. Less remembered than his clarion definition of "one beggar telling another beggar where to find food" is D. T. Niles's insistence on unapologetically engaging in the work of evangelism. "Evangelism is the call of the hour, as it has been the call of every hour when Jesus has been taken seriously. Sometimes world events spell out that call, while at other times the call comes through some person who has been in communion with his God. But at all times, when the call does come, it comes as a challenge and a compulsion."[23] At its most basic this involves our being consciously aware of the dictum of 1 Peter 3:15-16: "Instead, regard Christ as holy in your hearts. Whenever anyone asks you to speak of your hope, be ready to defend it. Yet do this with respectful humility, maintaining a good conscience" (CEB).

We must be unapologetically evangelistic, not for the sake of institutional maintenance nor less to limit the task to one branch of our current divide over LGBTQI/human sexuality issues. Profoundly and purposefully, we must engage in evangelism out of love for others and in commitment to the high call of Christ. The Great Commission is still in force: "Jesus came near and spoke to them, 'I've received all authority in heaven and on earth. Therefore, go and make disciples of all nations, baptizing them in the name of the Father and of the Son and of the Holy Spirit, teaching them to obey everything that I've commanded you. Look, I myself will be with you every day until the end of this present age'" (Matt. 28:18-20, CEB).

Unapologetic evangelism means we will engage in making disciples in answer to the Great Commission without apology or pause.

---

23 Niles, *That They May Have Life*, 11.

Bob Dylan's old album *Slow Train Coming* (in his Christian phase) has a classic line in the song "Gotta Serve Somebody": You're gonna have to serve somebody.[24] So it is, and we lift up Christ and him crucified and risen, the Lord and Savior of all humankind, who alone is worthy of highest allegiance and greatest commitment.

One element of this linkage must be the vital reconnection of witness in the deeds of love, justice, mercy, and verbal witness with a concomitant call to commitment to Christ as Lord. Lesslie Newbigin's famous dictum, "Words without deeds are empty, but deeds without words are dumb," applies at the deepest level of the church's life and witness.[25]

Currently the Church is blocked in its evangelism effort not by technique but rather by the deeper theological crisis exhibited by a vapid deism that renders any potent answer to the "why bother?" question raised by my brother and the legions of those who pursue gods of their own making. Alan Hirsch reminds us, "The desperate, prayer-soaked human clinging to Jesus, the reliance on his Spirit, and the distillation of the gospel message into the simple, uncluttered message of Jesus as Lord and Savior is what catalyzed the missional potencies inherent in the people of God."[26] Such an unapologetically evangelistic engagement will empower the Church today for tomorrow. It is no more nor less than the recovery of the original impetus for sharing the good news of Jesus Christ. It is no more nor less than the original explosion of the Methodist movement.

The Gathering

What will this look like? I offer one possible example through the emerging witness of The Gathering, a new faith community birthed

---

24 Bob Dylan, "Gotta Serve Somebody," *Slow Train Coming* (Columbia, 1979).

25 Lesslie Newbigin, *Signs Amid the Rubble: The Purposes of God in Human History* (Grand Rapids, MI: Wm. B. Eerdmans, 2003).

26 Alan Hirsch, *The Forgotten Ways*, 86.

partially within and without First United Methodist Church in Fort Worth, Texas.[27]

The Rev. Lance Marshall is a young adult who came to faith on his own. His initial appointment was not to a church but to a street. Seventh Street in Fort Worth, to be precise. It is a diverse setting abounding in young millennials—the upwardly mobile alongside those of lesser financial resources (including some homeless). Seventh Street is located on the edge of the Cultural Arts District of Fort Worth. He believes that this unusual start nurtured the practice of a high Christology because as he put it, "You have to really think through what you have to offer, an encounter with the living Christ."

Context

- The Gathering is a new faith community at FUMC Fort Worth, Texas. Worship began in February 2016. The Gathering currently averages 260–280 in weekly worship in two services.

- FUMCFW (First United Methodist Church of Fort Worth) has a multigenerational reputation for being theologically progressive.

- The current FUMCFW senior pastor has publicly shared a personal transition from a traditionalist to an inclusive stance regarding same-gender issues.

- The leader of The Gathering is a young pastor who has not publicly discussed a position regarding same-gender issues but offers to do so in a one-on-one conversation. *Pastor Marshall is emphatic about not talking about the issue through a power imbalance, by which he means from pulpit to pew. He believes strongly that such conversations must take place in the context of a more intimate dialogue and mutual reflection.*

---

27 Rev. Lance Marshall, pastor of The Gathering, a new faith community within First United Methodist Church of Fort Worth, Texas, has contributed substantially to this section of this chapter. My additions are in italics and come from an extensive interview with Rev. Marshall as well as personal visits to The Gathering.

In an interview, the pastor of The Gathering repeatedly pointed out that there is an ethos of repentance and conversion. He spoke at length about the struggle with idolatry (referencing explicitly the failures of moralistic therapeutic deism). Instead of asking people to "tweak" their lives, he noted that we "asked them to put aside shallow cultural values and embrace a deep and abiding life of discipleship following Christ as Lord." He says a lot, "Christianity is not just about being nice or learning be a good person." His own story is rooted "in an adult conversion to Christ as Lord." Pastor Marshall adds, "This was through non-Wesleyan evangelical voices. After conversion, I went on a search for the Christian community that was most resonant with me and I discovered Wesleyanism."

Mission

- The Gathering community focuses on evangelizing non-Christians and nominal Christians in their thirties and forties.

- This mission is particularly focused on young parents pursuing white-collar professional careers.

Mission, Vision, and Values

- The mission of the Gathering is to make disciples of Jesus Christ for the transformation of the world. Pastor Marshall has a strong call to offer the saving work of Christ. He reports extensive teaching on the doctrine of atonement. This is buttressed by what he calls a "clean understanding" of the need for salvation. In his explication of the atoning work of Christ, he speaks of the resurrection as God's ultimate "yes" to humanity's best attempt at "no." He often talks of atonement in terms of redemption and reconciliation.

- The vision of The Gathering is to create a community to which growing disciples love to invite their non-Christian friends and family.

- The values of The Gathering are hospitality, authenticity, engagement with the means of grace, and faith-sharing.

The congregation engages in regular prayers of confession that aren't about self-recrimination but honestly acknowledge where God is meeting us today. By way of example, Rev. Marshall shared the following: "When we were at our worst, you did not abandon us or turn away from us but joined us in power and presence of your Son, Jesus the Christ; not to forsake us but to reconcile and redeem us to right relationship with you."

The pastor repeatedly shares deep theological convictions based on *The Book of Discipline* and the Articles of Religion. In conversation he commented, "Bishop, I'm just very Wesleyan." What is laid out is a strong sense of core orthodoxy built on the classical doctrines of incarnation, sin, atonement (redemption and reconciliation), and resurrection. A strong doctrine of grace is always linked to Christ.

Holy Communion is offered every Sunday with the explicit invitation to encounter Christ at the Lord's Table. The young pastor commented, "It's a very evangelical communion." An explicitly traditional Trinitarian prayer is shared as a part of worship.

Results

- The Gathering features a core of long-term, committed disciples whose regular attendance and giving are the foundation of the community's stability and growth. This community ranges in age from mid-thirties to mid-fifties and is predominantly traditionalist.

- The Gathering is an engine for professions of faith from previously non- or nominal Christians, many of whom (*but not all*) hold inclusive positions.

- The Gathering also regularly attracts transfers of membership from committed disciples making their first move toward Methodism. Most of these transfers come from conservative and traditionalist denominations or independent Bible churches.

- The Gathering attempts to make disciples of Jesus Christ through creating an inviting and hospitable environment that introduces non-Christians to the means of grace. Weekly worship includes searching the scripture (scripture selections regularly reflect on thirty-plus verses), community prayer (prayers of the people), the Word proclaimed and Holy Communion. Each element of worship is explained, with the assumption that attendees might not have previously attended Christian services of worship. Topics of study and worship focus heavily on the felt needs of the mission field, particularly among educated parents pursuing significant family and career goals. The ethos of The Gathering is rooted heavily in the practice of repentance and conversion, calling on the congregation to recognize cultural pressures toward idolatry and to build their lives upon the foundation of the gospel of Christ Jesus.

- Attendees of The Gathering hold very diverse opinions toward same-sex issues, closely mirroring the diverse opinions in the mission field. Ft. Worth is simultaneously large, urban, educated, and youthful, while also reflecting the values of a deeply conservative county in a deeply conservative state. The approach of the pastor leading The Gathering regarding same-gender issues has been the following:

- To acknowledge that the entire Christian community is not of one mind regarding this issue, a reality that holds true in both The UMC and in The Gathering.

  — To acknowledge that both inclusive and traditional positions can be supported by arguments that are compassionate, scripturally sound, and promote the flourishing of all people.

  — To acknowledge that people of good faith can come to differing conclusions on these issues.

  — To teach that the root of the Methodist tradition is found not in doctrinal disagreement but in the serious commitment to Christian discipleship.

— To promote the practice of theological reflection by use of scripture, tradition, reason, and experience.

— To acknowledge that discussion of this issue is deeply sensitive, impacting the most personal aspects of faith, family, and love. As such, it is damaging to discuss these issues across power imbalances. Therefore, pastoral leadership will only address these issues in environments that can allow dialogue and reflection.

The result of this practice is a community that is successfully evangelizing its mission field and making disciples of Jesus Christ across a diversity of opinions and interpretations of same-sex issues. Exactly three people have requested to discuss these issues in a personal conversation with the pastor, and all three conversations simply hoped to ensure that an LGBTQI family member could attend The Gathering without being publicly shamed or humiliated. (Which, of course, was confirmed.)

An Easter Church

The current deep divisions in The United Methodist Church and growing refusal to abide by church law in any meaningful sense is inherently unstable. One of Lincoln's quotes echoes in the recesses of my mind, "A house divided against itself cannot stand."

The theological bankruptcy made evident by the ascendancy of moralistic therapeutic deism ushers in its own demise. Our current failure in the United States to define meaningful theological boundaries hollows out the witness of the current church. The aging of our membership presages an approaching financial cliff. Our institutional divisions lack sustainable coherence. The United Methodist Church as **currently constituted** will not survive, regardless of decisions at General Conference over same-gender issues.

And yet . . . God as Father, Son, and Holy Spirit is not done with us. In this battered and bruised world, a Methodist witness committed to the Wesleyan way of disciplined, obedient discipleship following Christ as Lord is more desperately needed now than ever. Something remarkable, and remarkably good, is taking place. God in Christ through the power and presence of the Holy Spirit is at work! Verses 19 and 20 of Isaiah 43 spring to mind: "Look! I'm doing a new thing; now it sprouts up; don't you recognize it? I'm making a way in the desert, paths in the wilderness" (CEB).

The context of this famous passage is significant. Israel has been defeated. The leaders are scattered into exile. It is hard to imagine life getting worse, let alone getting better. Yet in the darkness before the dawn, the prophet speaks of God doing a new thing. Allow me to suggest that something like this is again taking place under the Lord's presence and power through the Holy Spirit.

I hold to deep convictions not based on a Pollyanna optimism. We are not just an Easter people; we are an Easter church! There are signs of new life all around. The Lord God really is doing something new! McGrath is right: "The pursuit of orthodoxy is essentially the quest for Christian authenticity."[28]

> Embracing a full-blown, unapologetic, Wesleyan core, and classically orthodox Christian faith is the future.

Embracing a full-blown, unapologetic, Wesleyan-to-the-core, classically orthodox Christian faith is the wave of the future, however far out to sea that wave may yet be. It will scrub from the Church any pretense of Anglo-European and American dominance. The signs of its coming are scattered around us. The way ahead is difficult. It will call

---

28 McGrath, *Heresy*, 232.

for courage and sacrifice on the part of those who wish to be found truly and fully faithful.

We are duly challenged. Is Jesus Lord of our lives, including our professional work? Is this his church or a human institution? Make no mistake; the way is strewn with obstacles, but if this is the Lord's church, the gates of hell will not stand against it. Do you remember that marvelous interchange that takes place between Mr. and Mrs. Beaver and Lucy in C. S. Lewis's classic *The Lion, The Witch, and The Wardrobe*?

"Is he a man?" asked Lucy.

"Aslan a man!" said Mr. Beaver sternly. Certainly not. I tell you he is King of the woods and the son of the great emperor-beyond-the-sea. Don't you know who is the King of the Beasts? Aslan is a lion—*the* Lion, the great lion."

"Ooh!" said Susan, "I'd thought he was a man. Is he—quite safe? I shall feel rather nervous about meeting a lion."

"That you will, dearie, and no mistake," said Mrs. Beaver; "if there's anyone who can appear before Aslan without their knees knocking, they're either braver than most or else just silly."

"Then he isn't safe?" said Lucy.

"Safe?" said Mr. Beaver; "don't you hear what Mrs. Beaver tells you? Who said anything about safe? 'Course he isn't safe. But he's good. He's the King, I tell you."[29]

Questions for Discussion

1. Describe how the Holy Spirit is moving in your church/ministry setting.

2. How would you describe God's mission for your church? How can you live more fully into it?

---

29 C. S. Lewis, *The Lion, the Witch, and the Wardrobe* (London: Geoffrey Bles, 1950).

3. What do you believe Bishop Lowry means when he talks about an "orthodox" faith? What does he mean by the word *orthodox*?

4. Bishop Lowry says that there is "a growing sense among some bishops that we work side-by-side with two kinds of churches." Is your church more like the "fading, declining old mainline" or a "vibrant expression of the church"?

5. How does being a Christian affect your everyday living? What difference does it make to others that you are a Christian?

6. The UMC will always have differences. What holds us together or should hold us together as a denomination? What holds your church together?

7. When was the last time you spoke to someone about your belief in Christ? What makes it so difficult for some people to talk about their faith to friends, family, and others?

8. Read and discuss the Doctrinal Standards and Articles of Religion. You can find them in the 2016 Discipline, paragraphs 102–4 on pages 47–91. Did you find anything that surprised you?

9. According to Paul, what does it mean to be "set apart for God's good news" (Rom. 1:1, CEB)?

10. Why do many say that we are living in a post-Christian era?

11. How can a person be spiritual but not religious? Share about the people you know who might fit into the "nones" category.

12. Describe how your church offers Christ. What kind of witness does your church make?

13. Share a time when you experienced the love of Christ. How did you feel? How did your experience lead you to act differently? Why do you bother to be a Christian?

14. Imagine what it might be like to start a new faith community. Where might you start? Who would you choose to be part of the team?

15. How does your church engage God's mission for the church? Why is mission important to your congregation? What new directions might God be leading you? Your church? Our UMC?

16. What are the long-term prospects for your church in ten years? Twenty years? Fifty years?

17. If you knew you could not fail and had all power of heaven on your side, how would you engage for such a time as this?

3

Engage
for the Benefit
of the World

Grant Hagiya

Resident Bishop of the Los Angeles Episcopal
Area, The United Methodist Church

We face a critical junction in the life of our United Methodist Church. Because of the impasse on LGBTQI inclusion in our UMC denomination, our future lies in the balance. Unable to solve the theological and social problems of human sexuality through legislative means with our own General Conference structure, the church has turned to the Council of Bishops to deal with this adaptive challenge. The Council of Bishops in turn has created a thirty-two-member Commission on a Way Forward to bring recommendations and positive directions for the future of our denomination to a special called session of the General Conference in 2019. The Commission on a Way Forward has been meeting regularly in order to bring a viable proposal to the worldwide United Methodist Church in hopes of getting beyond our impasse. As a member of that Commission on a Way Forward, I remain optimistic that we will bring something of theological and ecclesiological substance to a church that remains hopelessly divided over this issue.

First, I think it is critically important to fall to our knees in humble confession before God that we are placing so much of our time, energy, and resources in moving the church beyond this impasse. As the younger generation both in and outside the church have often remarked to me: "Don't you realize no one cares that you are internally fighting over this particular issue?" In other words, for many of them, LGBTQI[1] inclusion is a given, and they do not understand why we are so divided over this issue.

Hence, first the need for confession. There are so many other critical missional issues swirling around us in the world: the rise of intolerance at all levels of our country; the blatant emergence of neo-Nazism and KKK racism; and a presidential administration that is determined to seal off our borders by scapegoating immigrants and threatening our very future by canceling Deferred Action for Childhood Arrivals (DACA),[2] thus deporting thousands of bright and energetic young people who have known only America as their homeland. We need to confess our own navel-gazing when the world is once again threatened by nuclear annihilation from a rogue nation and the immaturity of the threats by our own president in response to this crisis. How can we justify the internal attention to our denomination when the global ecological crisis continues to march on, and we see negative effects on the environment as evidenced by the prolonged rains brought about by Hurricane Harvey in the Southwest and the ongoing human needs that are its result?

To be truthful, my first prayer has been one of confession for the selfishness of The United Methodist Church that puts so much time and energy into our LGBTQI divide that it takes us away from the true mission that God has placed before us. In fact, that should be the

---

1 LGBTQI is a common abbreviation for members of the lesbian, gay, bisexual, transgender, queer, and intersex community.

2 An American immigration policy that allowed some individuals who entered the country as minors, and had either entered or remained in the country illegally, to receive a renewable two-year period of deferred action from deportation and to be eligible for a work permit.

starting place for the Commission on a Way Forward's recommendations: that God's mission supersedes everything, including our current impasse over human sexuality, which threatens to divide our church.

 The starting place for our mission is to be a proactive force for the betterment of the world.

So the starting place for our mission as United Methodists is to be a proactive force for the betterment of our world. We cannot retreat into our church buildings and stick our heads in the sand when the world is in such urgent and desperate need. The circumstances of our time call for an active, prophetic stand. For too long our United Methodist Church has been so preoccupied with our decline that our gaze has focused inward to the exclusion of the world around us. We have come to see the church so marginalized in human affairs that we really don't see ourselves as major players in worldwide decisions. We have come to lack so much confidence in the public square that we don't believe our voices or actions will make any difference. Instead of being more active and involved, we have retreated into our own denominational worlds and acted as though our United Methodist Church is the center of the universe.

I have continued to notice this reality during the two weeks of The UMC General Conference held every four years. When I was a delegate at the 2004 General Conference, there were rumors that the Bush Administration was planning an invasion into Iraq. I remember distinctly sitting through the proceedings of General Conference where there was not one prayer or deep discussion on the ethics of such an invasion. This painful example is the very self-centeredness of which I have been speaking.

We as clergy leadership do not need to be at our desks doing administration over the local church, huddled in denominational meetings that only focus on the future of our United Methodist Church, or sitting on the sidelines when the crises of our age are breaking out in our own neighborhoods!

We cannot afford to retreat into holy silence at this time in our world, not with what is swirling all around us. We must make prophetic stands, we must challenge the regressive movement of our present political administration, and we must do something to show our love of God and neighbor, especially when the weakest of our neighbors are being threatened. In my opinion, this is part and parcel of our mission from God.

The primary dilemma for us as United Methodists has been losing our mission focus. To quote my theological mentor, John Cobb:

> After the decline of Boston Personalism, we United Methodists have lost our way theologically. We are fragmented in the extreme, although a certain ethos, derived from our Wesleyan heritage, enables the denomination as an institution to hold us together . . . I prize this ethos. But without solid theological and missional underpinnings, the ethos fades. Our unity is fragile. There is a danger that the United Methodist Church as an institution is becoming an end to itself rather than the instrument through which we share in God's mission in the world. Despite the enormous needs of that world, we have been unable or unwilling to describe God's mission in it in a way that would clarify our own role in that mission.
>
> Perhaps more serious for us as Wesleyans than the loss of a unifying theology is this loss of a unifying mission, but perhaps we cannot know what we should be doing until we know better who we are.[3]

John goes on in his examination of Wesley in his book *Grace and Responsibility* to clarify that mission happens when we have a better knowledge about who we are as United Methodists. In a recent

---

3   John B. Cobb Jr., *Grace and Responsibility* (Nashville: Abingdon Press, 1995), 8.

discussion, he responded that Wesley's central mission can be sum-marized in one word: *love*. To paraphrase: If every local church truly focused on Wesley's understanding of love, we would find our cen-tral mission as a denomination.[4] However, as one quickly learns when studying with John, nothing is ever that simple, and this can be seen when he unpacks what he sees as Wesley's understanding of love as both grace and responsibility.

I would posit that this understanding of mission is in line with the premiere missiologist of our denomination and perhaps in all of the Protestantism in Boston School of Theology's own Dana Robert. To quote Dana:

> The idea of "mission" is carried through the New Testament by 206 references to the term "sending." The main Greek verb for "to send" is *apostellein*. Thus apostles were literally those sent to spread the "Good News" of Jesus's life and message. Notable passages in the New Testament contain explicit com-mands to go into the world to announce the coming of God's reign, such as when Jesus sent seventy followers to preach to the Jews (Luke 10:1-12). After his resurrection from death and appearance to Mary Magdalene and other women who had gone to his tomb, Jesus told the women to "go tell" his male followers that they had seen him alive.[5]

Thus, the notion of "being sent" highlights the current description of the Church and its movement from the "attractional" to the "missional" model. Being weighed down and tethered to buildings and professional clergy, we find ourselves in the old paradigm of attracting converts into the attractional church. This most often amounts to keeping old mem-bers in one place and being unable to avoid the natural decline in num-bers that comes when we "keep in" rather than "send out."

We contrast this with the missional model of bringing the gospel

---

4 Cobb: Personal Communication, September 8, 2017.
5 Dana L. Robert, *Christian Mission* (West Sussex: Wiley-Blackwell, 2009), 11.

message to those outside the church building through our many experiments with outreach. As an established denomination, we United Methodists find ourselves in a hybrid mode, where our existing buildings are forcing us into the attractional mentality, even while we know we must embrace a missional model because secular and younger people are not seeking to affiliate with any local church.

As I look at our United Methodist Church's future, I am not optimistic that the attractional model can be rejuvenated, as the march of secularization continues and the Pew statistics of the "nones" continue to climb. Our hybrid situation must give way to the missional model if we are to have a viable future. This also coincides with our return to mission itself as the central focus of our church's purpose and reason for being.

I have often posed to the seminary mission classes that I teach: "What if everything we did in the church was centered in mission?" How would this change the church and world? The response from the students is usually very positive and engaging, and their imaginations are spurred in a way that the institutional church does not often find.

So how would The United Methodist Church be different if everything we did started from the standpoint of mission? First, for the general church, we would move away from the time and resources spent on institutional maintenance to a commitment to mission itself. We would prioritize the sending mentality so that propping up the structure of the church would be a distant second. On the general church level we would spend less time and energy on data collection and maintenance, reform our method of apportionment collection, and spend less time and energy in general meetings at all levels of the church.

On an organizational development level, secular corporations and businesses must always balance their innovation and research with their internal management or maintenance, and for an organization to stay profitable the ratio is usually quoted at around 70 percent innovation and 30 percent management or internal maintenance.

Currently, our United Methodist Church is probably operating at the reverse ratio: 70 percent management and 30 percent mission. Some of us think we are probably running around 90 percent management and only 10 percent mission.

If we equate our church's mission to innovation, then we should be spending about 70 percent of our resources, time, and attention to mission itself, and only 30 percent to organizational management. Think of how our church would change if we made a commitment to this ratio.

 The church innovates best when engaged on the front line of mission.

I realize it is a big jump to equate innovation with mission, but my rationale for this paper is that the church is at its best in terms of innovation when it is on the front line of mission. When we are engaged in mission outside of the local church building, it often leads to the most adaptive and innovative solutions that the people of God can come up with. Think of any local mission trip or activity in which the church engages. There are always vexing problems that emerge, and through the ingenuity of the mission team—think of *The Wisdom of Crowds* by James Surowiecki—the group usually comes up with an innovative solution. Mission is not the only avenue of innovation that the church needs to be engaging in, but it is the most practical and easily attainable.[6]

On a jurisdictional conference level, we spend an inordinate amount of resources on what amounts to the election of bishops. I realize that some jurisdictions have the resources to do programming, but still the election of bishops continues to be the main goal of such conferencing. As a bishop, I don't think we are worthy of such attention, and I

---

6   James Surowiecki, *The Wisdom of Crowds* (New York: Anchor Books, 2005).

am becoming more convinced of the proposal by Russ Richey and Tom Frank that we should elect bishops at General Conference rather than at the jurisdictional level. Think of the time and money we would save if we didn't meet for jurisdictional conferences, or if we did meet we did it for the sake of mission in any given area. What if our jurisdictional members convened in one area to build houses, serve the poor, and evangelize neighborhoods? Instead of an internal maintenance focus, we would fulfill our missional calling of being sent to an area to share the gospel of Jesus Christ!

On an annual conference level, much of our time and resources are spent in organizational maintenance. I often think in the endless organizational meetings that we attend, my time would be better spent in teaching and preaching in our local neighborhoods and communities.

Our annual conference buildings have become the center of bureaucratic activity, housing finance, pensions, personnel, and organizational machinery. What if we turned those offices into cathedral centers that also served for worship, teaching, and the serving of the poor? How might our mission of the church be enhanced if, in addition to organizational maintenance, we reached out to our surrounding neighborhoods? What if we transformed our centers into "mission and evangelism posts," where we deployed clergy into missional fields, taught, and researched the most effective way to reach secular, ethnic, and young people in bringing them to Christ?

Finally, on the local church level, what if everything the church did was in the name of mission? What if we rediscovered the love, which Wesley envisioned and as John Cobb maintains, taught and modeled this love to our local neighborhood and community? Think of the discipling possibilities if we really taught and practiced prevenient, justifying, and sanctifying grace. We might have to come up with new names for these theological ideas to be relevant to younger generations; but the concepts are tried and true, and secular people are hungering for the meaning implicit in our Wesleyan theology and heritage.

As we move through our hybrid context, I have toyed with the concept of the local church as a mission outpost and our members as missionaries. It may put a new twist on what it means to be a member, and it definitely would strengthen our current definition of discipleship. What new models of mission at the local level might be unleashed if everything we did was motivated by mission?

Let me be clear: since my own field is organizational development, I am not against internal maintenance, and in fact no organization can sustain itself without attention there. However, our United Methodist Church ratio of mission to maintenance is in the opposite direction of what we need, running 70 percent management and 30 percent mission or innovation. We need to turn those figures around, and I believe our church can grow and thrive if mission becomes the central focus rather than maintenance.

In conclusion, I believe that a true rediscovery of mission provides the most viable hope for our United Methodist Church for the near and distance future. A true commitment to mission on the local, national, and international levels will invigorate our church and provide the most relevant means for secular younger people to connect with and believe in our central gospel.

I believe if our commitment to mission supersedes everything, it just may save our church from the impasse over human sexuality; but even greater, it may pave the way for true renewal and revitalization for our entire denomination.

Questions for Discussion

1. In what mission does your church engage?

2. Review what Bishop Hagiya says about missional and attractional models. What are some characteristics of a missional church? What are some characteristics of an attractional church? Is your local church more missional or more attractional?

3. Do you think The UMC has spent too much time on its own internal problems at the expense of ministering to the world?

4. Do you think issues surrounding LGBTQI inclusion are settled for younger generations?

5. Bishop Hagiya says that mission is the purpose of the church. Do you agree? Why or why not?

6. How much of your church budget is marked for mission and outreach? What percentage of your church budget is marked for institutional maintenance? What percentage of your church apportionments go for mission and outreach, and how much goes for institutional maintenance?

7. How would The UMC be different if we spend 70 percent of our budget on mission and 30 percent on maintenance?

8. How do you respond to Bishop Hagiya's call for a unifying mission for The United Methodist Church?

9. How does your church actively participate in district, conference, jurisdictional, or general church levels? How would you like to participate? Do you see ministry and mission beyond the local church as important? Why or why not?

10. What excites your church members about being United Methodist?

11. Bishop Hagiya says that "secular people are hungering for the meaning implicit in our Wesleyan theology and heritage." Is this true in your experience? Do you believe you know enough about our Wesleyan theology and heritage to make its case to people both inside and outside the church? What are some examples of how our theology and heritage meet the needs of people?

12. If you had all the power of heaven and earth on your side and knew that you would not fail, what would you do differently? What would your church do differently? What would our denomination do differently? Make a list and begin making a difference.

4

Engage
with Soul Curiosity

Bob Farr

Resident Bishop of the Missouri Episcopal
Area, The United Methodist Church

Introduction

A story involving an airplane trip is bound to appear every time I meet one of my bishop colleagues or hear a bishop speak. Spending so much of our time in our nation's airports, we make a lot of personal connections with the thousands of fellow passengers who, like us, are trying to make their way from point A to point B. Here's my latest airplane story.

I was headed to Atlanta doing what I normally do on planes—working through my reading list. The guy next to me turned and asked why I was reading this particular business leadership book. After exchanging notes on our reading material, he asked me what I do for a living. Deep breath. "I'm a bishop in The United Methodist Church." His reaction was no different than any other who hears my answer. "What in the world is that?" Trying to describe what a bishop is or does often goes poorly because: (1) I'm quite green in the role, and (2) it is really hard to describe what a bishop does to someone outside of our tribe. Try it.

This conversation started like so many others with strangers. These conversations are typically comfortable for me, offering me a chance to flex my extroversion muscles and do what I love best—share discussions about faith, life, and God. But this gentleman traveler turned the tables on me, and before I could even begin to gently ask about his life and work, he said, "So tell me about The United Methodist Church."

I've been a pastor for thirty-nine years. Rarely, if ever, do conversations get to the denominational questions within the first two minutes. So I shared about our church. He said he was a dropout Catholic and his wife, a disenfranchised Southern Baptist, to which I replied, "You'd make a great Methodist." I shared the idea of the *via media*, or the middle way, as part of our faith heritage. John Wesley's emphasis on the catholic spirit asks, can we be of one heart even though we are not of same opinion [translation mine]?[1] Typically, my role is asking all the questions, but he got inquisitive about my story. Finally, I got to ask *my* questions about his name, his life, and his work. He shared he had made a lot of money in life, retired, got bored, and got back into the corporate rat race to help a friend; yet, he still couldn't quite put his finger on what was missing in his life.

 Make a bridge between someone's
story and the spiritual life.

This was my opening. This is always the moment in a conversation evangelists are waiting to hear. It's the lynchpin of my work in the book with Doug Anderson and Kay Kotan, *Get Their Name*. How do you make a bridge between something in someone's story and the spiritual life? I said something like, perhaps it's the community of faith that's missing. He didn't miss a beat, launching into a number of

---

1   John Wesley, "Catholic Spirit" (Sermon 39) in *John Wesley's Sermons: An Anthology*, ed. Albert C. Outler and Richard P. Heitzenrater (Nashville: Abingdon, 1991), 301.

reasons why he and his wife don't go to church. Yet he still came back to the point of something substantial missing from their seemingly fulfilled life.

He surprised me with his next question: "If I were to come to a United Methodist Church, would they want to know why I have been gone?"

"No," I said, "if you show up at one of our churches, they will just be happy you are there."

"No, seriously, if I showed up at my church after being gone for forty years, they would want to know where I had been."

"No," I assured him, "I think they will just be genuinely pleased you show up that morning."

He didn't believe me. I tried to reassure him, while at the same time warning about the ability of thousands of United Methodist churches in the United States to execute with excellence. (Lord knows I've been in enough churches whose welcome committee was less than welcoming!) "We're pretty open to anyone who wants to worship with us," I said. This sparked another line of questioning. He shared that he owned a number of apartment buildings, and many of his best tenants were gay.

"Will your church be open to my gay friends?" he asked. I said, yes, I did not see why not. I shared that right then our church was having a lot of conversation about what this means for ministry, inclusion, and governance. "Oh no," he said, "I'm not sure how I feel about it, but I don't want to be a part of a church that doesn't welcome somebody."

After ninety minutes of conversation, including on our open communion table practices, he got to his final question: "If all you say is really true, where can I get me one of those churches of yours? My wife and I might like to go and try it out."

My mind drew a blank. I was a United Methodist pastor from Missouri flying to his hometown of Atlanta. Several seconds went by as my mind raced to think of any of the churches I had experienced in the Atlanta area.

"My friend Olu Brown has a church in Atlanta you might check out, Impact Church. It's in a warehouse. I can guarantee they will be open and welcoming to you and your wife. If you just show up, they will just be happy to have you." We exchanged business cards and got off the plane. I headed my way and he headed his.

 Find grace in someone's life and use it as a bridge to call attention to God's work.

I may never know if he walks into Impact Church. I may never know if he discovers what's been missing in his life. But, the conversation reminds me people have a deep curiosity in their soul about God, while at the same time are fairly disinterested in the local church. This is where the Church has an immense challenge and opportunity for relationship building. Being missional is being willing to engage in soul curiosity with someone you do not know and helping them connect to a faith community. God has placed that curiosity in people's souls. As Wesleyans we understand this as preventing grace—the grace initially pulling and drawing you toward the eternal. Our heritage also prompts us to experience God through community building. For Wesley, this included his methodical system of societies, classes, and bands. Part of our work as missional disciples is identifying grace in someone's life and using it as a bridge to call the person's attention to the work of God in the world. That airplane conversation may have been good for my seatmate's soul; I'll never know for sure. But it was definitely good for mine.

When we are not being missional and holding these types of life-giving conversations with others, we begin to dry up ourselves. Many of our congregations may be dead on Sunday morning in part because we are not experiencing soul-awakening conversations filled with grace and faith any of the other six days of the week.

I would be remiss if you walk away thinking conversations like this one happen all the time. They do not. Maybe, one in ten conversations. Some conversations end at "I'm a United Methodist pastor" with an eye roll and a stony silence for the rest of the flight. Some end with a lecture (from the other passenger) about how the world is going to hell and the apocalypse is nigh. However, this conversation was timely, given the broader conversation happening within our general church about inclusion. This man's questions about whether we will be open to him, a "backslider" according to Wesley, and to his gay tenants, got me thinking more deeply about the mission of God in the United States and the role of our United Methodist witness in that mission.

When the General Board of Higher Education and Ministry contacted me about offering thoughts for the second Colloquy between the church and the academy on how to reengage our Wesleyan heritage and participate in the missio Dei, I broke out into a cold sweat, as though I was back at Perkins School of Theology at Southern Methodist University. Anyone who knows me knows school was not a strength. Late in life I was diagnosed with a learning disability that explains so much of my struggle throughout school but came a bit too late to provide me with helpful strategies to make activities such as reading and writing easier. Like the story of Aaron and Moses in Exodus, I am a contemporary example of God placing people in your life to help bring God's hope for the Kingdom.

And yet, this chapter cannot be something that I am not. It is not an academic treatise on missiology. If I'm lucky it will be a practical, missional guide on how to share Jesus with others. My bias toward action will be quite obvious because, in my ministerial career, I have discovered my missiology through an experiential process. I believe we are all apprentice disciples of Jesus Christ. You cannot separate missiology and evangelism and discipleship. In fact, the genius of Wesley was that he linked them all together.

Mission, evangelism, and discipleship go together.

This chapter contains real examples taken from local churches. The work of God in the world is constantly in flux, and rather than being propelled up and out into the world by the Holy Spirit, it often seems that the Church is being dragged along, kicking and screaming, by that same Spirit. Suffice it to say, these examples are simply snapshots of how the Church is attempting to partner with the mission of God for the sake of our world. Are they the definitive solution for reaching new generations for Christ? Probably not. I've been at this for long enough to realize even the great ideas we consider now might be looked at with a criticism twenty years in the future as we learn more about human development and spiritual formation. Yet I do hope this chapter might be a conversation starter as we consider new pathways in our understanding and faithful practice of the missio Dei.

The Sending of God

The Church is the Spirit-led community of people confessing Jesus as Lord and living together as the body of Christ in the world. The Church is the primary vehicle for preaching the Word of God, administering the sacraments, and living out our mission. Yet, it is critical to remember, the Church does not have a mission of its own. It is God's mission for God's Church. As United Methodists, we believe the primary task of the Church within this mission of God is to "make disciples of Jesus Christ for the transformation of the world."

My understanding of how God's mission works in the world is largely drawn from Paul's Letter to the Romans. The entire Church responds to God's call to participate in this mission. "We know that all things work together for good for those who love God, who are called according to his purpose" (Rom. 8:28, NRSV). We respond, through our baptismal covenant, to live out this mission as we are "made to share in Christ's royal priesthood."[2] Missio Dei is best understood as the sending of God. Mission is, according to Karl Barth, an activity of God, and therefore the activity God does is sending Godself into the world. God sent the mission through Jesus, and the mission sends us into the world (Matt. 28:16-20; Mark 16:14-18; Luke 24:44-49; Acts 1:4-8; John 20:19-23).

Missio Dei as Wesleyan DNA

In a postmodern world, our culture is increasingly divergent; therefore, how we accomplish the Church's primary task is sometimes difficult to discern. It often feels as though we are grasping at straws. More often than I am comfortable, pastors and laity push back against the Church's mission with questions concerning what discipleship looks like or how we measure transformation. Wesley wasn't exactly concerned with what discipleship looked like. He was concerned with the practices of discipleship and believed that if you practice these disciplines faithfully, the resulting fruit will lead to transformation for you and the community around you. There is no one picture of discipleship. There is no one picture of transformation. Historically, we were called Methodists because of our methods, our practices. The three simple rules are practices.[3] Wesley's bands and classes were a means to hold disciples accountable to practices. It was and is an apprenticeship model.

This Wesleyan apprenticeship model emerged by turning to scripture for instruction. The early church made disciples as Jesus made disciples, by bringing others along on the journey—inviting them to share in the story of the faith (Acts 8), to practice "the apostles' teaching and fellowship," and "to the breaking of bread and the prayers" (Acts 2ff and 4ff, NRSV). It is an experiential model.

---

2   The United Methodist Publishing House, *The United Methodist Hymnal* (Nashville: Abingdon Press, 1989), 37.

3   For more about the three simple rules, see Reuben Job's *Three Simple Rules: A Wesleyan Way of Living* (Nashville: Abingdon Press, 2007).

What's Holding Us back?

Failure to engage in mission because of a claim of not knowing what the end product is supposed to be is simply an excuse. It prevents us from partnering in God's mission, but it's just one of many justifications holding us back from faithfulness. I see four additional obstacles preventing disciples from doing this work.

Obstacle #1: We Don't Want to Go to Bat for the Stranger

I have come to realize United Methodists are some of the nicest and kindest people. We love one another. We love to hang out together, eat together, and take care of each other when we are sick and hurt. If one of our churches gets damaged in a storm or fire, look out! United Methodists descend from all over to help out. While our people might go to bat for someone they know, I notice we struggle to do the same for those we don't know. Jesus scoffed; even pagans do that (Matt. 5:47)! As disciples we are called to serve the unknown.

It seems that many of Jesus's stories were about serving the unknown, disliked, and forgotten. He knew we prefer to care for our own and ignore those living on the edges of our world. Our culture and the US political climate definitely support that way of thinking, but it is in defiance of the missio Dei.

Obstacle #2: We Believe That Membership Has Its Privileges

Perhaps our greatest problem preventing us from sharing Jesus with others is one of the sacred cows in many of our congregations: membership. We need to get rid of membership. It denotes privilege. It breeds our family reunion–style worship and ministry activities. There is no scriptural basis for membership, whereas there is a scriptural basis for missionaries (Mark 6:7-13; Luke 9:1-6; Luke 10:1-12, 17).

Many of our new church starts come to the membership game late. In fact, we have had awkward conversations with the General Council on Finance and Administration regarding our largest churches (many of which have been planted in the past twenty years) with large average worship attendance but small membership numbers. These churches see membership as a deeply committed step into congregational leadership, instead of a call at the end of worship that ends with a handshake and a slap on the back (i.e., a "hug and mug" strategy). In these communities membership requires weeks, even months, of intense learning and accountability. This time of learning never ends, and the expectation is that if you commit to membership you fully embrace the practices of prayers, presence, gifts, service, and witness. You are expected to tithe and invite others into the community. Membership equates to leadership. You are expected to share your faith story publicly and be actively engaged in the sending of God into the world through your presence. You are to be a person of Christ in the world.

If the Church continues to keep membership, it needs to be extended to the most deeply committed leaders with high accountability. When the Twelve said they would follow Jesus, they lost stuff. They didn't gain privilege. Rather, they lost privilege and gained accountability. In our modern churches this might mean:

1. parking in the furthest spot from the front door;

2. sitting on the front row so guests can sit on the back row; and

3. missing worship to go serve another worship service or community needing the presence of Christ on Sunday morning.

Obstacle #3: Our Failure to Commit to Spiritual Practices

The third obstacle to living out the mission of God is our continuing failure to commit to spiritual disciplines. We need to trust that Christian practices make disciples, hold ourselves accountable to be faithful to our practices, and trust the Spirit is working through our spiritual practices to form us. As Paul reflected: "I planted, Apollos watered, but God made it grow" (1 Cor. 3:6, CEB). For Wesleyan Christians, these practices are prayer, study and reflection, communal worship, and holiness through service to and love of neighbor. The Holy Spirit has transformed me through these practices, and these means of grace are my personal examples of discipleship growth. I work out my salvation with others, my companions on the journey, who hold me accountable, affirm my gifts, and challenge my growth in relationship with God. This apprenticeship model transforms our hearts to be more missional, and in being missional we help transform the world.

Obstacle #4: Our Failure to Understand the Difference Between Being a Church with Missions versus a Missional Church

The fourth challenge to our work is our failure in understanding the difference between missions and missional. This is more than semantics. A church *with* missions needs to become a *missional* church. We are deeply entrenched in the notion of a "church with missions." I was raised and taught to create missions as part of the attractional model of church. This may have set ourselves up for this disconnection with the community. As a pastor I spent years and years doing missions *for* somebody but never even met "the somebody"! We sent team after team to international sites to build houses, failing to engage the local community and getting to know the people who would one day reside in the house. One of the licensed local pastors on my staff changed my perspective on missions. She said, "The task is the house. The mission is getting to know the people." I, along with my church, was so task-oriented we confused the to-do list with the actual mission. We were the mission, and we were sent to share ourselves with others as Jesus shared with the people he met on the road.

 We engage with soul curiosity only through relationship.

It only becomes missional when you engage the people through relationship. It is within that relationship that engagement with soul curiosity can occur. For a long time we mistakenly saw the missio Dei as a transaction rather than a transformational relationship. We need to move our churches from collecting things to building relationships. In Missouri, I want every one of our churches to adopt a school in their community; and I guarantee you the vast majority of them will understand that as, "Ah! We get to collect things!" The Lions Club can do backpacks. Tell me a name of someone you handed that backpack to; tell me something about the person's life and who God has created him or her to be. If you cannot, you are still doing missions rather than *being* the mission sent by God.

How Do You Show Jesus to Others?

Trying to discover the perfect way to engage in mission in the world seems like a waste of time to me. The real question might be, what does it mean to show Jesus to others in your neighborhood? How do you show Jesus to others? Simply put, we do this by making friends with others on God's behalf.

Make friends with others on God's behalf.

At one time, we were God's enemies, but God turned us into friends. Paul writes that God "gave us the task of making others his friends also. [God was in Christ making all human beings his friends.][4] God did not keep an account of their sins, and he has given us the message which tells how he makes them his friends" (2 Cor. 5:18-19, GNT). As friends and ambassadors of Christ, our work is not a call to judgment but an appeal to friendship. In order to make friends, the Church must be pushed beyond the walls.

I consulted on a Healthy Church Initiative (HCI) with a church that

---

4 Alternative translation. Could also read: "Our message is that God was making all human beings his friends through Christ" (2 Cor. 5:19, GNT).

hosted a weekly food pantry. After hearing about the ministry and learning the feeding program was largely transactional, our HCI team invited them to slow down long enough to ask each person, "May I pray with you?" The church did not respond well to this challenge, offering up the same excuses we hear from a lot of mainstream Christians— fear of rejection. But the church agreed to try it out. They discovered well over 50 percent said yes to offered prayer. The two-hour window for the pantry expanded another hour and then another as the church accommodated for relationship building. As it turns out prayer leads to conversations with the curious soul, and conversations lead to friendships. The church kept it up, connecting members of the congregation as prayer partners to clients in the pantry. Several months after the consultation, the pastor shared with me that for years the pantry had handed out invitations to their Christmas Eve service. No one ever came. That year, however, was different. When the pastor looked out into the congregation during the candlelight service, there were recipients of the food pantry seated on the front row next to their prayer partner.

The church learned that at the heart of moving from a church with missions to a missional church, they become a church with people at their heart. They are, in effect, moving from transactional ministry to transformational ministry. Engaging in soul curiosity is the stuff of transformation. Both parties in the relationship are transformed through this means of grace, a kind of holy conferencing.

Sharing Jesus with Others

Church wisdom used to claim we should get ourselves together first in order to go out into the world. We spent a lot of time focusing on ourselves—creating the best youth groups, the best choirs and musical programs, the best Bible studies, and the best family life centers. We did these things to attract people outside the church to come and be a part of our world. I think we could not have been more wrong. The

Church needs to go out into the world; then and only then will we get it together.

Additionally, the Church gets it wrong by thinking we have the market cornered on Jesus. Rather, the "Church is called to be that place where the first signs of the reign of God are identified and acknowledged in the world. Wherever persons are being made new creatures in Christ, wherever the insights and resources of the Gospel are being brought to bear on the life of the world, God's reign is already effective in its healing and renewing power" (¶102, *Discipline*).

We can learn about Jesus through the ways Jesus is already engaging and transforming culture. I continue to meet so many people who are soul curious. The prevenient grace of God has placed that curiosity within them. It's not about us bringing Jesus to the community but about us experiencing Jesus together with our community.

 It's about us experiencing Jesus together with our community.

Sharing Jesus with others is part of engaging in soul curiosity. It's also not that hard. Individuals and communities alike can follow the same three first steps to begin this journey with someone: (1) be willing to sacrifice your time (or agenda) to be with someone else; (2) pick up on the signs of prevenient grace working within someone's life and in their story; and (3) listen to the nudge of the Holy Spirit to build bridges of friendship between the person and Jesus. These are the essential steps in moving from acquaintance to authentic relationship. I spend a lot of time in my book *Get Their Name* on helping people become missionaries and trying to reclaim evangelism for the sake of the Kingdom. Critics of evangelism are in the right to critique shallow evangelism that tries to "sell" the Church to people outside the Church. God doesn't need our help "selling" the good news. By building real relationships with new people, we discover our experience with God is enriched.

We have a long way to go to move from a Church with missions to a missional Church, but as I travel around my state and throughout our connection, I see signs of hope and fruitfulness in our faithful witness. For the rest of this chapter, I will share some examples of missional outreach that I believe gets us closer to making friends for Jesus. I am sure each of these churches and their leaders will say that there is more work to be done as they partner with God for the sake of transforming the world. I also know there are countless other examples of this work being done.

From Transactional to Transformational

In the Missouri Annual Conference, we are attempting to live into the idea of being a missional conference rather than a conference *with* missions. For us, that means our twenty-year partnership with the North and South Mozambique Conferences through the Mozambique Initiative needed to move from simply a transactional model to a mutually beneficial relationship, which empowers both the Mozambican and Missouri churches. Admittedly, this is a work in progress. I have supported my own partner church, Nhachengue, through financial means for such things as a new well, a motorcycle for the pastor who visits two local churches over fifteen miles apart, and Bibles for its members in their local language. But I have done little to build a real relationship with the church or its people. The Mozambique Initiative is making progress in becoming more missional, and our ideas for the future excite me, because it really is about a mutually beneficial relationship. As we revised and recommitted ourselves to the Memorandum of Understanding with our Mozambican partners this past summer, we admitted that our salvation is tied together. As Archbishop Desmond Tutu describes the South African proverb of *ubuntu* ("I am because you are"), "My humanity is inextricably bound up in yours." We need one another to experience God's salvation. Future ideas for transformational mission together include pastor exchanges and shared learning between Mozambican and Missouri church planters.

In church planting, Missouri has experienced moderate success with multi-siting. But we had yet to reach our more economically depressed communities through this approach. That was until Grace United Methodist Church in Lee's Summit, Missouri shared a call to connect with the rural community of El Dorado Springs over an hour and forty minutes away from their main campus. El Dorado Springs is the largest city in Cedar County (population: 3,593). Forty-five percent of residents live below the poverty line. While a Methodist presence in El Dorado Springs has been around since 1881, in recent decades the church had been in serious decline.

The Kansas City suburban church might have simply sent money to this rural and economically challenged community. Instead, the church considered a realignment of their total resources in order to be missional to a particular community, and that meant people and technological resources, above and beyond financial ones. The main campus had to consider how to equip volunteers for service at both sites. They sent short-term missionaries to work with the El Dorado Springs campus. They identified a former tradesman feeling called to serve God, who moved his family into the community to serve as site pastor. The Grace pastoral staff offer him mentoring and continuing education as well as professional expenses. Taking care of administrative needs allows the site pastor to engage in soul curiosity with the community. Together, both campuses are learning their lives and ministries are intricately bound together.

Church in Real Life (IRL)

One of my favorite paraphrases of John's Prologue is "The Word became flesh and blood, / and moved into the neighborhood" (John 1:14, The Message). If Jesus, or the Word, in John's terms, is the mission sent to us and we are sent by the mission, we must ask ourselves what moving into the neighborhood looks like in our time. Being holed up in a nice stone or brick building with the doors closed tight might not be the kind of incarnational work John was writing about.

Several faith communities are figuring this out. Whether it be "Ashes on the Go" for commuters to begin their Lenten journey, bike blessings at the onset of summer, blessing of the animals in the local park, or theology on tap gatherings at the local tavern, some churches are figuring out that moving into the neighborhood means going to where the people are and engaging them in the stuff of life that interests them. One of the pastors at Good Shepherd began a small group at Pawn and Pint, a new business in Kansas City, Missouri that has board games and fantasy role-playing games available, and plenty of space to play them, for a five-dollar admission. He picked HBO's *Game of Thrones* as the entry point for a clientele interested in all things pop culture. The question of who will rule that drives *Game of Thrones* lends itself to parallel discussions about the Old Testament. As this chapter was being written, the business was welcoming the pastor back for a Star Wars Christmas to coincide with the release of the latest movie in the sci-fi franchise.

The method really doesn't matter. What matters is that the church is living among the people, not shuttered away, out of touch with the world. In a *Time* magazine piece published May 31, 1963, theologian Karl Barth said, "Take your Bible and take your newspaper, and read both. But interpret newspapers from your Bible." We have to read the Bible in one hand and the newspaper in the other. In today's world, this translates to: we must be the Church IRL ("in real life"). Union, in Dallas, is a coffee shop loving its neighborhood so much that its reason for existence is to "cultivate the divine spark in our neighbors for the good of the city and the world it inspires through outstanding coffee, robust community and engaging causes."[5] It strives to offer the most

---

5 "The Union Story," *Union*, accessed March 22, 2018, http://www.uniondallas.org/ our-story/.

generous cup of coffee by giving 10 percent of each sale to a local nonprofit organization. Their faithful witness in their community helps their neighbors become more generous. The coffeehouse's "Naked Stage," a storytelling and spoken word weekly event, creates awareness for social causes important to the people of their neighborhood. They are introducing their neighbors to Jesus and making friends in the process. Their brave and vulnerable witness of how the Spirit is working in their lives is making Jesus as plain as day to the soul curious.

Social Entrepreneurship

Social entrepreneurship has been around a long time. Since the beginning of time, people have pursued innovative ideas with the potential to solve a community problem. A church in St. Louis hosted a powerful small group on the ethical issues of poverty and the real-life experiences of their neighbors in poverty. So moved by this study, individuals from the group began relentlessly pursuing new opportunities to address the job and housing insecure population of the city. Out of that passionate pursuit, Bridge Bread and HomeFirst STL were born. Bridge Bread is a social enterprise designed to provide job opportunities for people experiencing homelessness. The goal of the program is to help the disadvantaged engage in a financially rewarding effort enhancing self-worth, promoting dignity, and enabling them to help themselves. HomeFirst STL supports people who once lived on the street by providing an affordable home, spiritual community, mentoring, and access to employment with the goal of ending homelessness. In both of these missional enterprises, the founding disciples had to delve into the realities of poverty experienced by their neighbors. They engaged in soul curiosity with someone they did not know, and in doing so, discovered the missio Dei together with the newly employed baking staff.

The Word at Shaw is part of a diverse and socially active community. Their missional approach to addressing home insecurity in St. Louis rests on Furnishing Hope, a ministry that partners with several homeless shelters in our neighborhood to provide furniture show-rooms. This quality shopping experience is designed for clients moving from a shelter into a new home and offers a dignified shopping experience for their clients as they begin making important steps toward financial stability.

Social enterprise provides some of the healthiest and strongest missional efforts internationally. Microfinance projects through the Mozambique Initiative are seeing the effect that dignified work can have on a community. The Dondo Motorcycle Taxi Project, supported by the church in Salem, Missouri, is one example of a financially sustainable project providing jobs and income for an economically marginalized community that was developed and maintained by the community in Dondo.

Mission with Teeth

For several years, we have invited Rev. Faith Fowler, pastor of Cass Community United Methodist Church and executive director of Cass Community Social Services, to speak to Missouri Conference pastors. Fowler and Cass Community Social Services is a Detroit-based agency taking seriously the church's role in making the lives of their community better. The nonprofit purchased twenty-five vacant lots from the city for $15,000. They built seven three-hundred-square-foot tiny houses with eighteen more on the way and offered new life, literally, in a neighborhood with one vacant, collapsing house next to another. There hadn't been a new building in this neighborhood since 1974.[6]

There are so many opportunities to build bridges with neighborhoods. But churches have to be willing to be vulnerable to get outside their comfort zone and follow Jesus into the neighborhood. The Episcopal Church of the Holy Communion in University City tapped into a

---

6   Cf. PBS Newshour, "Detroit's tiny houses give residents a home to rebuild their lives," August 22, 2017, http://www.pbs.org/newshour/bb/detroits-tiny-houses-give-residents-home-rebuild-lives/.

national model, Laundry Love (www.laundrylove.org), and introduced it to their local laundromat. One evening late in the month, the cost of doing laundry is on the church's tab. After listening to members of their community, the church's rector and leaders realized as the month grows longer, families on limited incomes find themselves stretched thinner. A free night of laundry, conversation with neighbors, children activities, and pizza dinner is one of the ways this church is showing Jesus to their neighbors.

Beyond the Walls

One of the most exciting missional ways churches are moving beyond their walls and connecting with their neighbors is through church-school partnerships. We have many churches that are working to move from transactional to transformational through intentional partnership with public schools in their community. The Gathering's Literacy Project in St. Louis focuses on literacy among kindergarten and first-grade students in Washington Elementary in the Normandy School District and Peabody Elementary in the St. Louis Public Schools District. Last year, they had over seventy volunteers working with students. This year, they hope to double their impact.

Rez Downtown is connecting with the Kansas City school district by using transactional ministry like backpack, school supply, and school uniform drives; and joy boxes at Christmas to build trust with school administrators, teachers, and parents so they can assist with the work of transformational change within the school. The church serves as a source of support for the schools they serve by hosting a bookmobile, incentive store, and end-of-the-year field day. They are moving toward a mutually beneficial partnership. Church volunteers are invited to strategic conversations and training opportunities hosted by the school district, and the relationship between the two matures and grows. The possibility for real transformation abounds.

Sometimes churches are uniquely gifted to address specific needs in the community, needs that are presented to us from outside the church. Live Well by Faith is a wellness program through the Boone County Health and Human Services Department for Black churches in the region. The program aims to address health disparities in minority communities through the church. At St. Luke UMC in Columbia, Missouri, the historically Black congregation prides itself on its "health evangelists" who educate people about the consequences of unhealthy lifestyles and encourage healthy eating. It is hard to be a health evangelist if you don't know the people with whom you are working. St. Luke is learning the hard work of relationship building saves lives and transforms the entire community. The integration of body and soul is a deeply Wesleyan idea. The opportunity for projects such as this one to engage in soul curiosity within someone they do not know is endless.

Local Impact Churches

Some churches are choosing to introduce people to the love of God by being Jesus's hands and feet through local impact ministries. Many of these churches are looking directly around the immediate area of the church to determine where they can have the most impact. Eureka UMC is located within the flood plain of the Meramec River. The river is the longest free-flowing river through East Central Missouri and has been a source of flood damage for many years. The church in Eureka shows up time and time again during flooding to work side by side with first and early responders. They know the names of their city officials and fire and police officials. They are building meaningful relationships. The city looks for the church to help coordinate its disaster response efforts. The church realizes some of the greatest impact they can have on their community is through the regular effect rising water has on their community.

One of the ways we share Jesus with new generations is just by showing up. When I consulted with churches in the Healthy Church

Initiative, I often heard the refrain, "We don't have any children in our church." I agreed, children may not be present in the church building, but there are a bunch of kids down the street at that school or in the park. What would it mean to have a small group of people from the church "adopt" a school sports team and cheer them on to victory? We read a lot about pastor-coaches/pastor-chaplains for the high school football team, but I bet the golf team would love similar help. Everybody loves supporting the big Friday night game, but do you think the junior high girls volleyball team would jump at the chance to have someone invest in their team as they travel from game to game? I bet so.

Expansion of Vocation

To share Jesus with others doesn't require a church council vote or even a launch team. I was recently reminded about the power of one missionary located in our most rural district. A twenty-seven-year-old lineman for the county electric co-op whom I'll call "Brad," first told me he had no intention of becoming a United Methodist pastor, because he couldn't see a place for someone like him (or his friends) in the church. He saw his "church" as his crew of apprentices and journeymen. "They are a rough bunch," he said. "But we are church to one another. Our work is difficult and dangerous, one wrong move and you're dead. If you don't think this is spiritual work, I don't know what is." Brad prayed with his crew and checked in on them and their families in the same way a class leader in Wesley's day might have done. Brad doesn't need to be ordained. He's doing the work of making friends on behalf of Jesus, and the Kingdom is better for it.

If only every baptized Christian would take seriously their baptismal vows as Brad does. What would it mean for the Church to expand its understanding of vocation so all baptized disciples understood their context as their mission field? Jesus's friends and family would grow exponentially.

Fall in love with Jesus. Help others fall in love with Jesus.

I am afraid we have taught people to fall in love with our churches rather than to fall in love with Jesus. We have given church to the next generation, and it has left them wanting. People are disinterested in just church but highly interested in spiritual things that can and will lead them into a faith community. If it's only about the organized church, when that church changes—the worship times change, the style of music shifts, the building falls down—some people cannot fathom connecting to another one. We have failed those people. Our hope is built on nothing less than Jesus Christ's blood and righteousness, as the song goes; it is not built within four walls and locked into the pews. For disciples like Brad, they have fallen in love with Jesus, not the church building or even the institution; so when he goes out to share Jesus with others, he is connecting them directly to Christ; and in doing so, he shares the community of believers with them.

Conclusion

This summer, I flew South African Airways returning from a visit with our partner conferences in Mozambique. The in-flight videos and magazine included the Zulu greeting I couldn't pronounce if it were not for the fact they played it over and over again during the eighteen-hour flight— *sawu bona*. *Sawu bona* means "We see you." Seeing someone in this context is more than the technical act of perceiving someone in your field of vision. It is a deep witnessing and conscious presence with another. I learned later the common exchange in the Zulu is to say, "*Sikhona*" or ("I am here") in return. According to Peter Senge in *The Fifth Discipline Fieldbook*, "the order of the exchange is important. Until you see me, I do not exist. It's as if, when you see me, you bring me into existence."[7] This exchange of greetings forms an agreement to explore the mutual potential and responsibility present in a given moment between people.

For United Methodists, what is the mutual potential and responsibility present between the Church and the world? There are so many people who are soul curious, soul hungry, and soul starved. Our baptisms call us to listen, engage, and create relationships with these people with grace and care. Our deployment into the world beyond our walls must be grounded in the Spirit and executed at the margins. Henry Rack argues persuasively that Wesley acted as a "cultural middleman" between Methodists on the one hand and clergymen and educated gentlemen in England on the other.[8]

As we consider how we might open new pathways in our understanding and faithful practice of the missio Dei, we are called to reclaim the position of cultural intermediary or translator in our world. Admittedly, this will be contextual. It will be different in every neighborhood. Some of us will be called to serve the working poor in our rural counties. Others will be called to serve the diverse and indifferent-to-religion next generations in our nation's urban centers. Still others will be called to be present with the affluent suburban housewives and househusbands. There are as many cultural scenarios as there are disciples and apostles. That's how God intended it. In commissioning the Twelve to go into the world, Jesus said, "Go, then, to all peoples everywhere" (Matt. 28:19, GNT). We are to go to *all* peoples everywhere. That means we need to become mediators to a whole lot of culture! In order to place ourselves in that middle ground, the Zulu concept of *sawu bona* might guide our footsteps. We must truly see the other in our community in order to respond faithfully to the mission of God.

---

7   Peter M. Senge et al., *The Fifth Discipline Fieldbook* (New York: Doubleday, 1994), 3.

8   Henry D. Rack, *Reasonable Enthusiast: John Wesley and the Rise of Methodism* (London: Epworth, 1989), 352.

Questions for Discussion

1. Share how you became a Christian. Who shared their faith with you?

2. Reread Bishop Farr's opening illustration about the man he spoke with on an airplane. Has something similar happened to you? If you were in Bishop Farr's shoes, how would you build a bridge with that person and the spiritual life?

3. What feeds your faith and enthusiasm for living?

4. Spend some time talking about how mission, evangelism, and discipleship go together. How is this true in your experience?

5. Reflect on the four obstacles that Bishop Farr outlines. Which, if any, are holding you and your church back?

6. How might your church move from being a church that does mission to a missional church? What are some characteristics that define what a missional church is? How does your church compare?

7. Discuss what Bishop Farr calls "soul curiosity." Give some examples of how a person engages with soul curiosity.

8. What does it mean to make friends with others on God's behalf? Share a time when you or someone you know made a friend on behalf of God. How is that different from just making a friend? Or is it?

9. How can we show Jesus to the world? To our neighbors? To our friends and families? To ourselves?

10. How does your church live in real life? What exciting things are happening in your church?

11. How can the church help people make their faith a priority?

12. If you knew that you would not fail and that heaven was on your side, what might you do? What might your church try?

13. Reread the section about Local Church Impact. What rings true in

your experience? What interests you about what some of these churches are doing?

14. On a scale of one to ten, how hungry is your soul and the souls in your church? Your family? Your neighborhood? Your town? Your school?

15. In your daily living, how do you show others that you love Jesus?

16. If you knew you could not fail and had all power of heaven on your side, how would you engage with soul curiosity? Make a list and begin to engage others.

5

Engage
with Strength and Generosity

Hope Morgan Ward

Resident Bishop of the Raleigh Episcopal
Area, The United Methodist Church

They go from strength to strength;
the God of gods will be seen in Zion.
—Psalm 84:7, NRSV

Strength

Following the Wesley Trail by car in the Pennines Mountains north of Durham, England, we came upon the villages of Ireshopeburn and Weardale. We sought the High House Methodist Chapel, the Methodist chapel in longest continual use in the world, gathering worshippers since 1760. The March wind was brutal, and it was difficult to push the car door open against it. The chapel appeared locked, but I made my way to a window and peeked in with hands cupped to each side of my face in an effort to see. A woman cleaning the church was greatly startled by my face in the window. She came to the door and opened it. I explained that we were United Methodists from the United States, following the Wesley Trail and interested in the church.

"Come in," she invited. We entered, and we were shown the pulpit where John Wesley preached thirteen times after the founding by Methodist preachers of the Methodist Society. Wesley came to Weardale in 1752, 1761, 1764, 1766, 1770, 1772, 1774, 1776, 1779, 1780, 1784, 1788, and 1790. On the wall was a pen and ink drawing of John Wesley riding into Weardale on his first visit. A crowd surrounded him in obvious welcome and excitement. Under the drawing were words from his journal, written on Tuesday, May 26, 1752.

> We rode hence to Weardale. I had been out of order all night, and found myself now much weaker. However, I trusted in the Strong for strength, and began preaching to a numerous congregation: and I did not want for strength, til I had finished my discourse; nor did the people want a blessing.

Wesley preached later the same day in Allendale. Surely God, the Strong, was with him. We were gifted by this serendipitous convergence of Bible study, prayer, and pilgrimage. God is indeed the Strong One.

Psalm 84 gives us words for our journey in mission, describing the strength of God and generously anticipating God's gift of strength to us. This strength is manifested in humility, gentleness, and compassion. God's dwelling place is lovely and gives joy, hospitality, and welcome.

> Even the sparrow finds a home,
> and the swallow a nest for herself,
> where she may lay her young. (v. 3, NRSV)

Receiving God's grace upon grace, God's welcome upon welcome, we extend grace and welcome. Christ's mission overflows out into the world. Psalm 84 continues:

> Happy are those whose strength is in you,
> in whose heart are the highways to Zion.
> As they go through the valley of Baca
> they make it a place of springs; . . .

> They go from strength to strength;
> the God of gods will be seen in Zion. (vv. 5–7, NRSV)

God is present in barren places, in the valley of Baca, a place of weeping and sorrow. Engaged in mission with others in such barren places, we experience the provenience of God. God is out front, anticipating, ever-present, at work ahead of us. In Christ's mission, we join all that God is doing to redeem, restore, reconcile, and heal. We are strong through the strength of God who is Strong.

A Strong Witness, Offered in Good Humor

Bill Wells served as a pastor in the North Carolina Conference with longevity and distinction, admiration and respect. He died at the age of ninety-three in June 2017. These segments of memorial tribute written in his honor describe the way God's strength works in us.

> William Miles Wells III of Laurinburg died on June 13, 2017. He was born in 1924 in Wilson. . . . He matriculated at Duke University, graduating in 1945 . . . where he claimed to have passed the mandatory swimming test only because he assured Coach Eddie Cameron that he did not have a job lifeguarding that summer. . . . He was a voracious volunteer and was honored in 1995 by the Governor of the State of North Carolina for his service. . . . Although he more than kept his promise to Coach Cameron and never worked as a lifeguard, he promoted water safety in a different way. For over twenty-five years, he taught swimming to fourth-grade students as part of a county-wide initiative in Scotland County to ensure that every fourth-grade student in the public schools has water-safety skills needed to prevent accidental drownings. (He finally decided to give that up at the age of 91.)

Bill Wells lived Christ's life the Methodist way, offering his life to and for others. There were no aquatics trophies adorning his study. However, as a mediocre swimmer, he offered himself in confidence, joy, and compassion. God's strength works in us as God's strength worked in Bill. Our participation in Christ's ministry is like leaven in a loaf of bread, as salt in a stew, as a mustard seed planted in the soil. We remember Jesus's parable of the sower. We fling seeds. Some seeds fall on sandy soil, some fall on a rocky path, some become food for the birds. However, some seeds fall into good soil, and this is enough. God brings a great and surprising harvest. This is the good news, alive in Bill Wells, alive in us.

 The Methodist way of life: offering our life to and for others.

Initiative

God is Creator, Savior, Sustainer: God initiates, and God with great patience seeks and welcomes, always giving life and breath. God is not overwhelmed. God is ever-present, ever-seeking, ever-embracing, ever-loving.

Hurricane Matthew devastated Lumberton, North Carolina in October 2016, with heavy rain flooding the city, inundating five thousand homes. Gary Locklear, North Carolina Conference lay leader, offered this witness: "I was in my house for three days, in the darkness without electricity or running water. Then I decided to get up and go out and get to work."

The Easter imagery is unmistakable. Jonah was thrown up from the belly of the great fish to the safety of the shore. Lazarus was called forth from death and unbound and let go. Jesus was raised from death behind a sealed tomb. We follow this pattern as we are called forth from darkness, disaster, and grief to light, healing, and hope.

Gary became immediately the teller of the story of devastation. His homeland, Robeson County, was devastated. Like Nehemiah, he embraced the mission to restore his home. Like Nehemiah, he prayed and circled the area. Like Nehemiah, he beckoned people to rise up and build.

The response has been amazing. Neighboring United Methodist friends in the Western North Carolina Conference were immediately present, generous, encouraging, and resourceful. Prayers, volunteers, supplies, and financial gifts have continued to flow since the October devastation.

In March 2017, Bishop Leonard Fairley celebrated his sixtieth birthday with a host of those he leads in the Kentucky and Red Bird Conferences. Ninety came from Kentucky to North Carolina, driving the long distance to sleep on a church floor and to labor together restoring households. At a joyful celebration of our United Methodist connection, United Methodists from Kentucky and North Carolina feasted, celebrating the ties that bind us in Christ's ministry. The Kentucky and Red Bird Conferences brought with them a gift of $20,000 to be used in home restoration in Robeson County.

The story of creation is celebrated in poetry and in prose in the first chapters of the Bible. God is the great initiator. In the magnificent creation poem of Genesis 1, we see clearly initial goodness: God creates and calls all that has been created good. In the captivating creation story of Genesis 2–3, God creates humanity, places humanity in a verdant garden, and then charges humanity to name the animals one by one. God cares for community by creating a partnership, and even seeks those who are tempted and who choose unwisely. God calls us by name, and we hide in fear and shame. The journey of the Bible is the story of God who consistently reveals divine love and purpose to us, page by page—through history, poetry, wisdom, visions, prophecy, genealogy, gospels, letters, theology, parables, biography. God is consistently the creative initiator of newness, life, birth, and resurrection.

 Mission is Christ's life in us.

Made in God's image, we initiate. We connect and we create. Mission is Christ's life in us, connecting with others. In the language of

Thomas Kemper, the General Secretary of the General Board of Global Ministries, mission is "from everywhere to everywhere." Like God who initiated all things in creation and who creates continually to our surprise and delight, we engage with others and find God alive, present in them and alive in our midst.

Sufficiency

The Duke Endowment is helping us understand what is necessary for vital mission. The Duke Endowment was founded on December 11, 1924 by James B. Duke. In his book on the Duke Endowment, Robert F. Durden wrote, "The true fountainhead of the multifaceted philanthropy embodied in James B. Duke's charitable trust lay in North Carolina Methodism." His Indenture of Trust established the Endowment and charged it to work with four named universities, hospitals, programs that promote child well-being, and rural United Methodist churches. The Rural Church program area of the Duke Endowment funds ministry—with an emphasis on developing clergy leaders, fostering strong congregations and outreach in the area of literacy, affordable housing, and food and hunger. Continuing to analyze the data related to the efficacy of financial support, the Duke Endowment now states clearly that its grant-making has shown that the construction of buildings does not lead to growth; in fact, over time, worship attendance and giving decline. However, grants made for outreach programs are far more likely to foster engagement that leads to increases in worship attendance.

Our greatest resource is the heart and spirit of people. Christ's mission has become in too many hearts and minds entangled with church buildings and property. In the United States, we have in most places abundance of property and buildings, funded and built by those who have gone before us. We have spaces and equipment and resources that we hold in trust to be used faithfully and well. It is essential to offer guidance and help to lay and clergy leaders as we seek to claim and use these resources.

Church Transformation Ministries in the North Carolina Conference guides congregations in a process of discernment toward a faithful and fruitful future. The director of Church Transformation Ministries collaborates with an advisory team and works closely with the cabinet in identifying churches that are ready to clarify options and discuss their future. Some congregations have limited capacity for turnaround and sustainability, no longer able to effectively use property and other resources for mission. The process of discernment includes prayer, Bible study, truthful naming, and visioning for the future. The central question becomes, "How might we use who we are and what we have for mission in the years ahead?" It is our great hope that considering this question may lead to rebirth and renewal, in faithful and expansive ways. Churches may be reborn and continue in vital mission. Churches may faithfully decide to connect in congregational life with other churches. Churches may decide to offer assets as a legacy gift to the continual effort of creating new places for new people to become disciples of Jesus Christ.

 How might we use who we are and what we have for mission in the years ahead?

It is essential that we look with new eyes to assess faithfully the assets available for ministry. New life can come in surprising places as we claim strength, use the assets we have, and reach out to all the people near our church property, buildings, and missions.

All God's Children United Methodist Church in Aulander, North Carolina celebrated two decades of ministry in 2017. In 1997 Reverend Laura Early read the Bishop's Initiative on Children and Poverty and sensed God's beckoning call. She met with Bishop Marion Edwards and others in conference leadership, sharing her vision. She wanted to gather a people who would love children. She wanted to mitigate the impact of poverty upon their lives. She asked to be appointed to the small economically distressed town of Aulander. She requested permission to use the Aulander United Methodist Church, which had been closed for six years.

Today, All God's Children is a place of dynamic worship. It is also a place of possibilities where children are mentored, tutored, and encouraged and where women engage in micro-businesses such as sewing. Dynamic partnerships have been created with others, including the Duke Endowment, the North Carolina Annual Conference, the Good Will Foundation, the Peak United Methodist Church, and the Beacon District. Growing ministries continue to beckon, strengthen, and connect people in Aulander. Teaching and coaching flow as student interns engage with people in the community for summer or school term placements. The North Carolina Annual Conference is called repeatedly to ministry with the poor through the life and ministry of All God's Children United Methodist Church.

Generosity

In the midst of a worship service at Chestnut Street United Methodist Church, I whispered to Pastor Herbert Lowry, "How many people have been helped in Hurricane Matthew recovery so far through Chestnut Street?" My question was inspired by the leadership of Chestnut Street in responding to Hurricane Matthew. The church welcomes, shelters, and feeds volunteers continually while housing on the second floor of their facility the Disaster Recovery Ministries staff in Robeson County.

Reverend Lowry whispered back, "You will have to ask upstairs." Indeed! We imagine heaven as "up," so the imagery is delightful. The numbers helped are known only to God, written in eternity. The response of the pastor was, however, in itself a demonstration of generosity. An amazing, effective, and persevering leader in the mission of hurricane recovery, Reverend Lowry could easily have been ready

98

with a large number. However, his focus is on people, one by one. He welcomes volunteers, delighting in their generosity, presence, and labor. He comforts many who lost their homes and possessions in the flooding. He develops resources, communicates great need, and offers wisdom. He is willing to do small things well, over and over, helping one person after another. It never occurs to him to memorize numbers.

Others attend to the important ministry of administration. The number "upstairs" that day in the Disaster Response Office was impressive: 2,600 volunteers offering time, skill, and labor; $3,900,000 saved in home restoration; 122 households restored or on the way back home. People pray, travel, give, work, and share life with us generously.

The exploration of personal and collective generosity is delightful. We tell our personal stories of the experience of generosity. In the community of the cabinet, we share our memories—the people and places and circumstances that have taught us to trust God's abundance. The stories are delightful: the memory of a mother selling her wedding ring to finance her son's final year of college; the memory of a mother baking a neighbor's favorite cake and watching the neighbor eat the whole cake himself (!); the memory of a father keeping church-offering envelopes on the top of his dresser in the bedroom; the memory of an optometrist discounting eyeglasses when the son of a seminary student broke his brand-new ones. At cluster charge conferences, district superintendents tell their stories of being awakened to the power of generosity.

The storytelling goes wider, as church leaders tell their stories and invite circles of storytelling. During Lent, the invitation to write meditations sharing stories of generosity was extended. Every day during Lent, a story was sent out by e-mail to all who receive conference messaging and was posted on the conference webpage. Conference T-shirts bear the words "Generosity in All Seasons." For this season of our life together, we focus on generosity—in all places, in all creation, in all seasons of life, in all seasons of the liturgical year.

> The experience of generosity is at
> the heart of the mission of God.

The Bible is alive, vibrant, and teeming with stories of generosity. Generosity is everywhere in scripture. God creates all that is out of divine generosity. God leads us from slavery to freedom through generosity. God speaks generously through the prophets. In Christ, God's generosity is complete and abundant. As we celebrate the Lord's Table, we prepare through thanksgiving, remembering that Jesus lived divine generosity: welcoming outsiders, eating with sinners, healing the sick, feeding the hungry, and raising the dead to life. The early church experienced the generosity of God in Pentecost, receiving in full measure the Holy Spirit. Peter, Paul, Lydia, and many others experienced abundance of life and fullness of joy. God in generous love continues to embrace all people and all creation. The experience of generosity is at the heart of the mission of God.

Abundance

Jesus fed a multitude on a hillside by the Sea of Galilee. This memory is powerful for the church. All four Gospel writers tell the story of abundance. Thousands eat through the power of God and the offering of loaves and fishes by a child. God's nature is abundance, and we share that divine nature when we experience God's abundance and trust it for ourselves and others.

West Robeson United Methodist Church, a rural church of small membership, experienced the loving care of many people after Hurricane Matthew devastated their community. When Hurricane Irma bore down on Florida in September 2016, the people of West Robeson remembered God's goodness and abundant provision. They knew that people would be evacuating north, nearby, on Interstate 95. They anticipated that people left Florida in haste, perhaps without adequate provision or money.

The idea emerged: take food to the North Carolina Welcome Center on Interstate 95. They moved their Sunday worship outside and into action, taking hot dogs and bottled drinks to the Welcome Center. They asked if they could set up grills to offer food to travelers evacuating. Permission was granted, and they prepared to welcome and offer food and comfort. A simple sign was created out of brown cardboard: Free food for Irma Evacuees—West Robeson United Methodist Church. People began to stop for sustenance. Stories were shared of leaving quickly without adequate provision or cash. Other people saw what was happening. Cars began to roll through, offering twenty-dollar bills. Someone posted pictures, and the mission went viral. Television crews appeared from Lumberton and Fayetteville, interviewing for the evening news. Hundreds of people ate and drank and gave thanks.

The great interest and energy generated a second idea. The people who evacuated would be returning south on Interstate 95. The need continued, so West Robeson set up the sign and even greater provisions the next Sunday on the southbound side of the highway. They were fortified with gifts from neighboring churches. Hundreds stopped to eat and drink and give thanks on their way back to Florida. Letters of gratitude from travelers—and relatives and friends of evacuees—flowed afterward into the church, the district office, and even the bishop's office. Another observation is noteworthy: within weeks, the worship attendance at West Robeson United Church rose from thirty-five to ninety.

A small child offered Jesus meager provision: five loaves and two fish. By the Sea of Galilee, Jesus took the gift and multiplied it. The disciples and the people were amazed as they ate their fill, gathering baskets of over-supply. This story was central in the life of the early church. All four Gospels tell the story. Jesus is described as taking, blessing, breaking, and giving the bread to the multitude. These actions were repeated in the last supper of Jesus the night before his death. These four actions were repeated in Emmaus as Jesus is recognized in the breaking of bread. These four actions are described in Paul's instructions for Communion in the Corinthian church.

The miracle continues to happen. God's generosity continues to flow to us and through us to others. As we share in Christ's ministry, we live the fourfold action of miraculous feeding on the hillside and at table. Hot dogs are taken, cooked, blessed, and given. As this happens, we are on the Galilean hillside, in the Upper Room, at the table in Emmaus, and with the Corinthian church. God's abundance continues to flow.

Confidence

Late afternoon on Saturday, August 12, 2017, we turned on our television and saw news from Charlottesville, Virginia. Moments later I received a text from a clergy in our conference. She asked, "Are you going to write something today about Charlottesville?" I heard urgency and anxiety in these nine words. I heard a desire for help in responding faithfully, effectively, prophetically, helpfully. I heard a plea for help in crafting her own words. I heard desire for faithful confidence.

As I watched the violent racism, I brought to mind all the clergy and laity across eastern North Carolina, who would be leading congregations the next day. What would be most faithful and helpful in this moment? I decided to text an encouraging message to a number of our clergy serving in university communities.

On Sunday afternoon, I received this responding text from one of those university clergy, Rev. Heather Rodriguez, lead pastor at Duke Memorial United Methodist Church near Duke University in Durham: "Your text reminded me that we are not alone and it held us accountable to lean into the messiness and light of yesterday's tragedy in Virginia. This is what I hope we did. Thanks." Indeed, we are not alone. Community, encouragement, and connection are sources of confidence in God's presence and guidance, essential in this time of great contention, chaos, uncertainty, and anxiety.

On Monday I received e-mail. In one, a layperson wondered with great distress why his pastor did not speak of Charlottesville, even in a pastoral prayer. In another, a layperson wondered with great distress why her pastor called her a racist. I suspect that in the first instance, the pastor did not know how to speak into racism in his congregation or was fearful that speaking into racism would provoke dissention and criticism. I suspect that in the second instance, the pastor tried to speak into racism faithfully and threw a match into the dry kindling of congregational denial, fear, anxiety, and anger.

That same day I did write of Charlottesville and offered a prayer for use in local churches. My intent was to help clergy and laity find even better words and ways to engage the realities of race, history, and memory. The church is called to speak into real circumstances with courageous strength and courageous humility. It is essential that we create conversation circles where our life stories might be spoken and heard. Paths are needed toward confession, repentance, forgiveness, and reconciliation.

We can be confident in the difficult work of anti-racism. An anti-racism team is now formed in every district. These leaders are planning and leading opportunities for laity and clergy to engage the history of our communities, our state, and our nation. Journeys offered and engaged include trips to the new Museum of African American History and Culture in Washington, DC; the Greensboro Civil Rights Museum; a remarkable exhibit on race at the North Carolina Museum of History; "freedom rides" to places of importance in our civil rights history; forums and seminars on multicultural realities and the history of Hispanic, Native American, African American, and Asian culture in our state. Clergy leaders making the journey from commissioning to ordination go on a "freedom ride" each year, learning the history of African American people in North Carolina. The journey begins with enslavement and the Christianity of the slaveholder and moves to emancipation, fusion government, violent establishment of Jim Crow laws, the civil rights movement, and the Moral Monday movement.

Local churches are aligning themselves in this educational effort, creating opportunities for Christian formation, multicultural experience, and anti-racist witness.

We configure other courageous conversations in our shared life. In January 2017 we invited laity and clergy into conversations, creating Circles of Abundant Grace for the second full week in the new year. District leaders discerned locations, and fifty conversation leaders—trained by JustPeace two years earlier and commissioned at the 2015 Annual Conference for leadership in times such as this—facilitated the listening and speaking. Over seven hundred laity and clergy participated, even with attendance-decreasing snowfall. Guiding principles were established, helping all to be confident of the benefit of the conversation. Whenever the conversation happens, it is the right time. Wherever the conversation happens, it is the right place. Whoever participates in the conversation is the right person.

The template for conversations was simple, hospitably opening space for speaking and listening. Each conversation began with centering prayer, self-introductions of all present, the reading and hearing of Philippians 2:1-14, and sharing of the context of the gathering within the movement of The United Methodist Church from the 2016 General Conference into the Commission on a Way Forward. Two focusing questions were offered to prompt discussion: (1) What do you want to say and hear in The United Methodist Church concerning human sexuality? and (2) How do you think The United Methodist Church can move forward in its witness on human sexuality?

Strength and courage are required to create spaces for difficult conversations. There are persons in any gathered circle with deep hurt, differing opinion, and varying hope. Care and preparation and expertise in leadership of these conversations is essential. When conversations are well led and courageously engaged, Christ's mission flows through us. Abundant grace is present as we gather, welcome, speak, and listen to one another.

Creativity

In Wilson, North Carolina, a dozen committed leaders created Living the Word, an intentional, interracial covenant community of meeting, reading, learning, and growing. The group was made up of clergy and laity, half African American and half white, in a place and a time of racial division. They studied scripture. They read and discussed important books such as *The New Jim Crow* by Michelle Alexander. They wrestled intellectually and spiritually with ideas and with each other. A wonderful and challenging commitment emerged out of two years of deep engagement with one another. They decided to do something to impact the stark reality of the low rate of success of African American male high school students.

They created *A Gentleman's Agreement,* a collaborative effort with Wilson Public Schools, to offer these students support, mentoring, and cultural experiences. The name emerged as the young men articulated that "we are born boys, we grow to be men, but we choose to be gentlemen." The first cohort of these students has mentors for regular engagement and experienced journeys to the National Museum of African American History and Culture in Washington, DC, *The Lion King* on Broadway tour in Durham, and the National Civil Rights Museum in Memphis, Tennessee. The vision continues to unfold: the hope is now to create scholarships for alumni of *A Gentleman's Agreement* to go on to higher education.

Across North Carolina, United Methodists have joyful and creative engagement with public schools in our communities. Through Congregations for Children, or C4C in our common parlance, we invite United Methodist people to "walk across the street" or "drive down the road" to a nearby public school. All children are welcomed at public schools, and we seek to be connected in mission with all children and their families. We initiate helpful partnership by asking public school principals a simple but profound question: "How might we help you?" Then we listen.

C4C has become a strong partnership of the North Carolina and Western North Carolina Conferences. To date, 83 percent of the eight hundred churches in the North Carolina Conference self-report partnership with a nearby public school. C4C has four clear goals: (1) providing basic necessities such as backpacks of school supplies, weekend food packages, winter coats, or other needs identified by teachers; (2) helping every child learn to read by providing tutors, giving books for children to have at home, offering after-school programs and summer reading camps to push back summer learning loss; (3) engaging significant adults in the life of every child, especially men, as mentors and loving role models; and (4) helping United Methodist people understand the impact of poverty on the lives and learning of children.

Reverend Elizabeth Polk and the people of Ellerbe United Methodist Church have created a contagion of mutuality in their partnership with the local elementary school. As the church of small membership responded to the expressed needs of the school principal and teachers, their enthusiasm was infectious, and their neighbors became partners in mission. The town librarian offered the resources of the library in the effort to help children learn to read, including a remarkable summer camp pushing back "summer learning loss." The mayor offered his strawberry patch, launching a strawberry festival.

Reverend David Hutchins and the people of Red Oak United Methodist Church led the entire Red Oak community in renewed engagement with children. The church organizes a 10K walk/run that raises $10,000 annually to support a summer reading camp for sixty children, twice the average worship attendance of the church. Jacob's Friends, a group for children with atypical needs, was created by a member of the church, a mother of a son with special needs. At a recent gathering, one hundred people gathered in a celebration for thirty children and youth with special needs in this rural community.

Winstead United Methodist Church in Wilson has consistently over eighteen years claimed a mission with a nearby elementary school. Mentors, particularly men, have established long-term relationships with boys who have no father or significant male adult in their lives. The church has acquired a house near the school, and they are preparing the house to be a center for parent education, English as a second language courses, and other initiatives.

We continue to learn the importance of relationship. Training is offered to churches as they are led into partnership with schools. At one training session in a high poverty county, the excellent trainer asked forty United Methodists gathered for training two questions. The first question elicited a simple yes or no: "Did you know that all the children in this county are on free or reduced-price lunch?" Every person in the class answered yes. The second question probed deeper. "Do you know the name of a child on free or reduced-price lunch?" No one in the room could answer yes. One pastor volunteered this commitment. "I do not know names now, but I will know the names of all the children in first grade this year," she said.

Mission is essentially relational. John Wesley insisted that direct engagement with those in need is a means of God's grace to us. He went farther, saying that he would prefer neglecting the sacrament of communion than neglecting the grace that comes from direct, face-to-face, relational mission among the poor. His observation is true and abundantly helpful. Engagement with children, their families, and their teachers is a means of grace to us. We have experienced remarkable alignment of effort. The annual conference continues to communicate C4C has a priority focus of mission. An annual summit of C4C leaders from churches and from public schools in July is an occasion to celebrate progress and to learn new ways to begin, engage, and grow in partnership. The four priorities—basic needs, reading, engagement of adults, and understanding the impact of poverty—are now our mantra as we create partnerships with public schools.

C4C offers sufficient structure as creativity is fostered. Each partnership is as unique as a fingerprint while connected to partnerships in other places. Through C4C, we are experiencing a helpful balance of mutuality and originality, blueprint and improvisation.

Conclusion

These observations and experiences are grounded not in optimism but in strong Christian hope. We are people of restoration and reconciliation and resurrection. Violence, injustice, fear, conflict, and anxiety persist. However, Christ has chosen us, and we have chosen Christ. We are people who continue to experience grace—grace going before us, grace surrounding us, and grace guiding us onward. We continually choose Christ's ministry, as it overflows in vitality, life, and impact. God is at work in the world, restoring all things to the divine intent, through generosity and sufficiency and abundance. Confident in the sufficiency of God, we go forward toward the promise: *from strength to strength.*

Questions for Discussion

1. Share a time when you or someone you know had to rely on God's strength.

2. Share a time when you or someone you know served in mission. What was it like? What happened?

3. How does God take the initiative with us? Discuss the meaning of prevenient grace.

4. After reading Bill Wells's memorial tribute, how might you want to be remembered?

5. How might we use the resources we have as well as who we are as individuals, families, and churches for mission in the future?

6. How does mission energize you? Your church?

7. Share some examples of generosity. How do you think Jesus modeled generosity? How does your church model generosity?

8. Read 2 Corinthians 12:8-10. What does it mean that God's grace is sufficient? How might that fact play out in your everyday life?

9. How do you respond to Bishop Hope Morgan Ward's examples of churches in mission?

10. When people experience violence, what words of hope can Christians bring? How can we, as faithful followers of Jesus, help those who may have lost confidence in God and God's goodness?

11. Courageous conversations are usually hard. How can Christians mediate the presence of God when we discuss difficult topics and have conflicting viewpoints?

12. What is the difference between optimism and hope? Between wishful thinking and hope?

13. Where do you see God at work?

14. If you knew you could not fail and had all power of heaven on your side, how would you engage with strength and generosity? Make a list and begin.

6

Engage
to Multiply
Our Witness

Robert C. Schnase

Resident Bishop of the San Antonio Episcopal
Area, The United Methodist Church

First, I want to express my appreciation for the opportunity to participate in the Boston University School of Theology Colloquy. I particularly want to thank the General Board of Higher Education and Ministry and the Association of United Methodist Theological Schools for hosting conversations about the future of The United Methodist Church as we seek to find a way forward at this critical time.

Thank you for breaking out of the usual constraints of the academy by inviting practitioners into the conversation. For this moment in the life of the church, we cannot merely rely on the academy to glean from the past what we ought to do in the future. Nor can we simply rely on the experience of those on the front lines of ministry. We depend upon the insights and reflections of the academy as well as the experiences and perceptions of practitioners, not only to help us determine what is essential to who we are and for what we need to carry us forward to further the mission of God, but also to determine what we must leave behind. None of us has all the answers.

> The church has no mission except
> the mission of God in Christ.

Missio Dei

Second, I appreciate the focus on the missio Dei, the mission of God, rather than merely on the mission of the church. The language of "the mission of the church" helps in some practical ways to organize our work and to inspire the church to action. However, to focus too narrowly on the mission of the church runs the risk of seeing the church as an end in itself. Missio Dei reminds us that the church has no mission except the mission of God in Christ. It provides more clarity about our source and our end. Missio Dei rescues us from preoccupation with ourselves and reorients us toward our neighbor and toward the transformation of the world.

Missio Dei also appropriately highlights the "sentness" of the church. To say that clergy in The United Methodist Church are called to be sent is not merely a nod to our Wesleyan notions of itineracy; rather, it finds its roots in the revelation of God in Christ, who came "not to be served but to serve," not to pursue his own will, but "the will of him who sent me" (Matt. 20:28; John 4:34, NRSV).

Jesus did not sit passively waiting for people to come to him. In obedience to God he stepped into the lives of people of all types: Jews and Gentiles, women and men, neighbors and strangers, the up-and-coming, and the down-and-out. Jesus crossed borders of social propriety, engaging the woman at the well, the grieving soldier, lepers at the margins, and tax collectors in their homes. He crossed literal borders, sending his disciples to be his witnesses "in Jerusalem, in all Judea and Samaria, and to the ends of the earth" (Acts 1:8, NRSV). He nudged people across the borders in their own imaginations, describing a Samaritan as the unexpected bearer of grace in a story of compassion. Jesus's understanding of the mission was expansive, active, and driven by the grace of God.

> God's grace propels us and compels
> us to go places we might never go.

To focus our attention on the missio Dei rightly pushes us beyond the notion that we fulfill our task when we pour all our efforts into making a congregation so attractive to unchurched people that they will come to their senses, show up in our place of worship, like the music we prefer, and agree to our way of doing things. It breaks through our passivity by pointing us to the active verbs of the gospel of Jesus Christ: go, teach, pray, give, heal, love, forgive, baptize, obey. The missio Dei reminds us that God's grace propels us and compels us to go places we might never go if left to our own preference and convenience. In a broken world, no church can sit still when drawn into the missio Dei. The mission of God gives the church an ever-restless quality, pushing us outward into the world that was loved by God so much that he gave his only Son. Thank you for framing the topic with the missio Dei.

Missional Purpose

I originally hesitated when I was invited to serve on the Commission on a Way Forward. I didn't want to pour myself into the task of "fixing a problem" or of designing a new "restructuring plan" that would likely be rejected by the Council of Bishops, the General Conference, the Judicial Council, or any of a dozen other entities that do better at restraining creativity than at adapting our message to the mission field.

After consideration, I agreed to serve on the Commission on a Way Forward because I love The United Methodist Church, and I believe The United Methodist Church offers a unique voice to the Christian witness that reaches people other branches of the Christian family cannot reach. I agreed to serve because I truly do believe that, by God's grace, we can discover a way forward that does not repeat some of the difficult pathways our sister denominations have traveled as they have addressed controversial social issues.

However, I had to be convinced of the missional reason for having a Commission. What won me over was the *Mission, Vision, and Scope Statement* of the Commission provided by the Council of Bishops, which reads in part, "The Commission will design a way for being church that maximizes the presence of a United Methodist witness in as many places in the world as possible, that allows for as much contextual differentiation as possible, and that balances an approach to different theological understandings of human sexuality with a desire for as much unity as possible." The statement also invites the Commission to seek to "do this work with complete surrender to God's unlimited imagination and kingdom purposes."[1]

Our work is missional. The fundamental task of the Commission is not to overcome an impasse that has lasted for more than forty years. Our task is to consider creatively how to multiply our witness and maximize the impact of the mission that God has given us.

This is why the Commission's work is important and why what happens at General Conference matters. It's not about saving an institution. John Wesley didn't try to save an institution. Rather, he tried to multiply the Christian witness by innovative experiments and new models of organizing people that maximized ministry. Having a Commission is useless unless it focuses on the mission of God rather than the survival of the church.

Mission and Imagination

Our early history as Methodists is heavy-laden with terms like *discipline, rules, minutes, standards,* and *plans.* The very name *Methodist* finds its roots in the chiding about our forbearers' focus on order, consistency, repeated practices, common patterns, and organization.

I want to express my appreciation for several long-standing conversation partners, including Bishop Janice Huie, Dr. Gil Rendle, and Rev. Tom Berlin.

1 "Commission on a Way Forward: About Us," The United Methodist Church, accessed October 4, 2017, http://www.umc.org/who-we-are/commission-on-a-way-forward-about-us.

When we concentrate too much on the organizational nomenclature we've inherited from the Wesleys, we overlook the unfettered creativity, freedom, audaciousness, and imagination they brought to the task of fulfilling the mission of God through the Methodist movement. The Wesleys could be stiff and eccentric, but they were also wildly imaginative regarding the mission. Every innovation the Wesley brothers supported was mission-driven, including many of the elements that still order our church.

What was the purpose of an *annual conference*? John Wesley did not create churches, preaching houses, societies, classes, and bands so that one day he could form a conference. He conferred together with his preachers to strengthen the work and multiply the impact of the preaching houses, societies, classes, and bands. Early conferences focused on how best to do the work God entrusts to us, considering how to "save our own souls and those that heard us,"[2] learning "what to teach and how to teach it,"[3] and sharing biblical and theological conclusions that compelled Methodists into service.

The purpose of the *itineracy* was to multiply the Methodist witness. Preachers went wherever their overseers discerned they were needed to maximize the witness rather than instinctively following their own preferences. As Mr. Wesley wrote, "What is sufficient call to a new place? A probability of doing more good by going thither than by staying longer where we are."[4] He moved preachers so the mission field experienced a mix of talents "needful for beginning, continuing, and perfecting the work of grace in a whole congregation."[5]

---

2   John Wesley, "Thoughts Upon Some Late Occurrences," *The Works of the Reverend John Wesley*, A.M., vol. 7 (New York: J. Emory and B. Waugh, 1831), 309.

3   John Wesley, "Minutes of Some Late Conversations Between the Rev. Mr. Wesleys and Others," *The Works of the Rev. John Wesley*, vol. 8 (London: John Mason, 1830), 275.

4   John Wesley, "Minutes," *The Works of the Rev. John Wesley*, vol. 9 (New York: J. and J. Harper, 1826), 369.

5   John Wesley, "A Letter to the Rev. Mr. Walker," *The Works of the Rev. John Wesley*, vol. 10 (New York: J. and J. Harper, 1827), 208.

The reason for *General Superintendency* was to develop, oversee, and deploy leadership to support the mission. The use of *lay assistants* in teaching, preaching, and leadership multiplied the Methodist witness. The practice of *field preaching* reached people the existing church could not reach. The *publication* of hymnbooks, the rewriting of Christian classics, the creation of a *Discipline*, and eventually *ordaining preachers* and sending them to America—all these innovations and experiments and departures from institutional tradition found their purpose in multiplying the mission of God through the Methodist witness.

The idea of *connectionalism* itself was not a bureaucratic strategy that Wesley adopted to maintain and save an institution. Rather, it was a spiritual reality Wesley discerned: that our responsibilities, callings, and accountability extend beyond the walls of a congregation and are interwoven into a larger expression of the body of Christ. Conference relationships and connectional systems helped Methodists accomplish together much more than they could do apart from one another.

How much of what Mr. Wesley accomplished in his lifetime was done to accommodate the institution of the Church of England? How much of what he did was done to adapt to the mission field?

Mr. Wesley, as innovator, concerned himself little with perpetuating an institution that had grown disconnected with significant portions of the society. Instead, he directed the people called Methodists toward those unreached or underserved by the institutional.

At the Edges

Picture a congregation as a set of concentric circles, with a small circle in the middle, surrounded by a larger circle, and then a larger circle still, and so on. The small inner circle represents the insiders, including the pastor, staff, and a few laity who know nearly everything that happens. The next larger circle includes the elected chairpersons, team leaders, and teachers of classes, the directors of music. The next circle includes those who participate in small groups and serve on teams and volunteer for committees and sing in choirs. The next larger circle includes those who regularly attend worship. Another larger circle includes those who feel that they belong to the church even though they attend sporadically. At the outer edge of this largest circle, a margin delineates those who belong to the church from those who have no relationship with the church. We hope the margin is permeable so that new people can enter the community of faith easily and we can reach across it daily.

> A role of leadership is to direct the
> church's attention toward the margins
> and therefore toward the mission.

The church fulfills the *missio Dei* at that margin. It's at that margin that people who belong to the church engage other people beyond the church with the evangelistic mission of the church, inviting them to the spiritual life. It's at the margin that we offer our ministries of mercy, service, and justice to relieve suffering, seek peace, and reconcile people. God's mission through the church is not fulfilled at the center in council meetings, planning retreats, and finance committees, as important as those are. At best, these meetings prepare us for the mission and point us to the mission field. The role of leadership in the church is to direct the attention of the church toward those margins and therefore toward the mission.[6]

Now picture an annual conference the same way, as a set of concentric circles. At the center are the bishop, the cabinet, the chancellor and lay leader, the conference staff. The next larger circle includes other leaders of the conference, lay and clergy, who chair committees,

---

6 Paraphrase from Robert Schnase, *Just Say Yes: Unleashing People for Ministry* (Nashville: Abingdon Press, 2015), 9.

lead task forces, prepare reports, and complete studies in service to the conference. The next circle represents the clergy of whatever status, deacon, elder, local pastor, or lay minister. The next circle includes all the voting members of annual conference, lay and clergy, youth delegates and district representatives. Finally, the largest circle includes the congregations, faith communities, campus ministries, and conference service projects. It's at that outer edge where a conference fulfills its purpose by engaging the world through congregations and faith communities that impact the world and bear witness to God's revelation in Christ.

It's not at conference meetings that the mission is fulfilled. Conferences are not on the front lines; congregations are. Conferences do not console the bereaved, feed the homeless, offer recovery ministries, or perform baptisms; congregations do. Conferences, at best, prepare and equip and teach and provide resources to multiply the number of fruitful congregations. They help those who help and serve those who serve.

The *Call to Action*, the initiative from the Council of Bishops leading up to the 2012 General Conference, challenged the denomination to redirect more resources toward increasing the number of vital congregations. The recommendation did not represent a dangerous veering toward congregationalism so much as a realistic assessment that if congregations continue to weaken and die, then so does our witness and our ability to influence the culture around us with a prophetic and life-sustaining word.

The focus on increasing the number of fruitful faith communities was a denominational attempt to fulfill what Francis Asbury persistently pursued in the late eighteenth century when he wrote, "We must draw resources from center to circumference."[7] He recognized

---

7 Cited in John Wigger, *American Saint: Francis Asbury and the Methodists* (New York: Oxford University Press, 2009), 9.

the need to make the Methodist organization more adept at expanding into newly populated areas if the church was to remain faithful to the missio Dei in the United States.

Drawing attention to the edge, to the margin, to the mission field is work that belongs not simply to conferences and congregations but also to the academy, to our general boards, our councils, and our foundations.

This work also belongs to the Commission. How do we design a way for being church that maximizes the presence of a United Methodist witness in as many places in the world as possible, that allows for as much contextual differentiation as possible, and that balances an approach to different theological understandings of human sexuality with a desire for as much unity as possible? Our work is missional.

Mission Field Thinking

Wesley's practical genius resulted from his persistent attention to the mission field and his willingness to adapt his practices according to the context. United Methodism requires a similar reexamination of our practices, systems, and structures to address the many and varied mission fields God has entrusted to us. We must apply such thinking to our own challenges today.

A colleague tells the story about how her understanding of the appointment process evolved with each quadrennium she served as a bishop. In her early appointive sessions, when the cabinet and she agreed upon sending a pastor to a particular church, she found herself picturing the pastor as he or she receives the news of the new appointment. Would the pastor receive the appointment as good news? Feel happy, affirmed, recognized? Or would the pastor feel angry, unappreciated, misunderstood, punished? Reflecting on those early years of her episcopacy, she realized an unspoken underlying theme and value to the appointive process was Happy Pastors.

At a later point in her work, and after she became better acquainted with the churches and lay leadership of her congregations and of their expressed needs, she found herself picturing how the news about the appointment of a particular pastor would be received by the congregation. Would the congregation feel they had been heard? Would they be excited and positive and supportive? Would the appointment be perceived as a good match? The unspoken underlying value became Happy Churches.

As she became better acquainted with the communities, the diverse neighborhoods, and the unmet needs of the people surrounding congregations, her view shifted again. She began to think differently about the purpose of the appointive process. She began to picture the unreached people in the vicinity of a congregation, those the church had never ministered to, perhaps because of shifting ethnic or economic demographics. Which pastor might she send who would have the gifts, experiences, skills, and inclination to connect the congregation to the mission field, to make a difference in the lives of those within the church's reach? How might the community be different because of this pastor's appointment? How will the lives of people be changed, including the lives of people who currently do not even know the church exists? The underlying value evolved from Happy Pastors to Happy Congregations to Mission Field Thinking.

The developing notion of itineracy in the bishop's story grows from a maturing appreciation for the connection between missional awareness and the contextualization of ministry. It also derives from a sharpened awareness that *mission field* is not an abstract idea; it is actual people with distinctive needs in a particular place and time, and that the mission fields served by most of our churches are changing. When we pay little attention to the context, we grow insular, disconnected, and irrelevant to the world around us.

Wesley broke out of the constraints of the academy of his day and moved beyond the institution of the church when he experimented with field preaching, straining his relationships with his bishop, his fellow clergy, and the institution of the church. His emerging awareness of the unmet needs of the mission field resulted not merely from a change of heart but of location, of place. He stepped away from the academic cloisters and the Church of England pulpits into the open fields. He moved beyond the homes of clerics and Oxford dons and into the homes of the poor. He crossed social and economic borders to learn about the daily lives of people who did not enjoy his privilege and status. Because of these actions, Wesley began to see the world differently. He realized the mission field was changing, and a singular focus on parish churches would no longer be sufficient. He trained his eyes to willfully observe the people whom the Church of England barely noticed.

Likewise, for the Commission on a Way Forward to achieve more than "resolving an impasse," we must be willing to move beyond the constraints of our institution once more, doing so with a concern for as much unity as possible within the church and as much impact as possible in the mission field. While the Commission's work requires the Council of Bishops' approval and the support of General Conference, the missional target is to equip congregations to reach their mission fields where our churches are now and will be in the future.

Contextual Differentiation

The formation of The United Methodist Church in 1968 merged kindred branches and righted many wrongs, including the long-standing injustices of the Central Conference in the United States, the fruit of blatantly racist strategies. But the shifts that took place between 1968 and 1972 also introduced layers of prescribed structural uniformity.

We began to treat congregations, districts, and conferences as interconnected widgets that must all operate in uniform fashion or else the connection would suffer. This uniformity reflected corporate and governmental models that reached their apex ten to twenty years previously. The organization of The United Methodist Church required every church to have the same administrative board structure, the same council on ministries, the same work areas that perfectly aligned with similar work at the district, conference, and general church level. *The Book of Discipline* required the same structures with the same names for every church no matter how large or how small, all for internal purposes, and with no variability derived from the mission field. Context did not matter. Unity relied upon common structures more than a common understanding of mission.

How do I become, as Paul suggests, a Jew to the Jews, a Gentile to the Gentiles, and "all things to all people, that I might by all means save some" (1 Cor. 9:22, NRSV) if I'm held accountable for doing the same things in the same ways, no matter the context? Effective ministry always occurs in creative interchange with the mission field, the incarnational identification with those we seek to serve. The mission field gives our expression of the gospel its particular contours and distinctive language. It is not simply the needs of the community but the calling of God, missio Dei, that captures the heart of a congregation to go forth to serve the community in particular ways that cannot be prescribed entirely from some distant denominational headquarters. The answer to "Who is my neighbor?" (or more aptly, "Who is my neighbor *now*?") determines how my ministry will take a different form than yours.

Space and Relationship

The Commission hears a yearning from both traditionalists and progressives for more space. More space means more structural distance from people who practice ministry differently or more autonomy to adapt practices to the context that may not be requested elsewhere. Traditionalists do not want to be required to participate in same-gender weddings, the ordination of LGBTQI persons, or the financial support of a bishop in a same-sex marriage. Progressives want space to freely exercise ministries that include same-gender weddings, the ordination of LGBTQI persons, and the same-gender marriage of clergy. Central Conferences want space to shape conversations about sexuality according to their national context and without replicating whatever requirements shape the US church. Centrists want to give space as generously as possible without compromising core identity and mission.

Is space merely another word for contextualization and mission-field thinking? Clearly, the tools necessary for ministry are different in the rural Midwest than in New York City or Mozambique or Norway. Or is the idea of needing more space fundamentally a challenge to the unity of the church, a concession to our inability to get along with one another or to support one another's ministry? Is figuring out how to live with more space in our connection a missional task, or work that undermines our witness?

How much space is needed by traditionalists, progressives, and centrists? Too much space, and in effect, we create two or three denominations with distinct episcopacies, general conferences, and annual conferences that while sharing a common Wesleyan heritage would have little structural relationship. Less space might mean various expressions coexisting under one umbrella, created in some manner that allows conferences or churches or pastors to choose to affiliate with an affinity group within a single denomination. Little or no space will lead us to enforcing uniformity.

What does space mean? Some space sounds like a nod to contextualization. Too much sounds like separation.

Dr. Charles Wood, in his contribution to a previous Colloquy, describes the notion of subsidiarity as "the principle that decisions are to be made and policies adopted on the lowest possible level,"[8] not giving higher authority functions the functions that local people can assume. He also describes reconciled diversity as the way in which "churches with historically conflicting ways of ordering themselves

---

8   Charles M. Wood, "Appendix A: An Ecclesial Vision for The United Methodist Church," *Unity of the Church and Human Sexuality: Toward a Faithful United Methodist Witness Study Guide* (Nashville: GBHEM Publishing, 2017), 193–94.

can recognize each other's order as legitimate, though not binding on themselves."[9]

The notion of a less centralized, more flexible, more contextually agile, more differentiated church challenges many United Methodist leaders who are accustomed to establishing rules meant to apply to everyone everywhere. Perhaps now we have an opportunity to resolve the mistakes of 1968–1972 when we leaned too heavily into uniformity, an error we have kept repeating ever since.

Maximizing our capacity for contextual differentiation so that congregations, pastors, or conferences have permission to adapt their practices to the mission field brings its own set of challenges. If we are not careful, the more diverse the expressions of Methodism and the more latitude we provide for the principle of subsidiarity, the more given we become to division and polarization.

Rooted deep in our Methodist ethos is the desire not only for space and contextual freedom but also for relationship and connection. We're going to need more space, and we're going to need relationship. We're going to need more freedom to differentiate as well as a deep sense of connection. We want to be contextual, and yet we yearn to be one.

Perhaps space and relationship are not opposites. They represent a tension to be held rather than a conflict to be resolved.

We can still be one and be contextual. Wesley did it. He stayed connected, and he stayed contextual. And we see the examples of unity and contextuality in our Central Conferences, who operate with the essentials of our tradition but vary in practice in order to best serve their contexts.

Reframing Critical Questions

The questions we on the Commission are asking are not the same questions many others are asking around us, such as "Who is right and who

---

9   Wood, "Appendix A," 95.

is wrong?" or "How can we all be together in common agreement?" Unity is not agreement. We will never have agreement, and an understanding of unity that requires or expects agreement is naïve and illusory.

Even bishops, or maybe especially bishops, will have to understand that unity is not uniformity; it is not agreement, and it is not achieved by lifting structural connection higher than purpose or mission. Connection must always be in service to the mission, as we saw in Mr. Wesley, rather than the other way around. We may have to redefine unity within the scope of our purpose. The Commission may provide an answer that the church is not asking for, because the church prefers resolution rather than tension.

The Commission has been asked to make practical decisions for missional reasons. Among the critical questions are the following: What kind of church will we be? What do we need to carry with us as we navigate any changes that might come? What do we need to leave behind? What is essential to our identity and practice? And what must we be willing to let go of to fulfill the mission of God in this moment of the church?

The Missional Church

As the missio Dei draws us to the edge where the church reaches the mission field, we inevitably experience a tension. At the edge, we must hold on to what is central to our faith while also embracing contextual differentiation. As soon as we approach the edge with the treasure that has been entrusted to us, what comes from the other side are questions of faith being asked in contextually different ways. The authentic core of faith and the authentic experience of the context create the tension. As we learn to live with the tension without trying to resolve it all the time, we thrive.

A missional church repeats the innate tensions of identity and purpose that have existed from our earliest creeds. The church is one, holy, catholic, and apostolic—all four—never merely one against, or at the sacrifice of the others. As John Deschner, my systematic theology teacher from years ago, used to say, "Robert, it's not multiple choice." We can't push aside the oneness or the holiness of the church in favor of an apostolic church, just as we cannot sacrifice the apostolicity to preserve its oneness.

This tension is particularly acute for bishops, individually and as a council. Bishops play an historic and critical role as visible leaders of the oneness of Christ's holy church while creatively and incessantly focusing the church's energies on the mission of God in Christ. They are expected to exemplify and protect the holiness of the church, the transcendence that does not bend with the trends of culture. They are asked to bear witness to the catholicity of the church, seeing ourselves in relationship with every other part of the body of Christ, including multicultural and worldwide expressions of the church. And they are expected to exhibit fidelity to that same proclamation and mission of those apostles sent out to perform a task given them by Christ, the missio Dei, with the authority and freedom to spread the good news of God's grace.

Bishops give visible expression to the oneness of the church. They also are entrusted with drawing the attention of the church to that contextual edge where we fulfill our mission, the missio Dei.

The task of finding a way forward has been given by the General Conference to the Council of Bishops. I pray the Council discovers the courage and discerns the wisdom to make practical decisions for missional reasons, as Mr. Wesley taught us to do.

Questions for Discussion

1. Reread Bishop Schnase's section "At the Edges." Take a minute to map out your church. Who is at the center? Who are in the various circles? Who are at the edges?

2. Bishop Schnase says that a role of leadership is to direct the church's attention toward the margins. Is this true in your context? How might leaders do this effectively?

3. How is your church engaging the margins? To what effect?

4. In what ways can churches multiply their witness?

5. How can we communicate to people at the edges and margins that the Christian life is fruitful? How do we express the fruitfulness of our faith? Is your church fruitful?

6. Many churches deal with multiple contexts in terms of beliefs, preferences, opinions about social issues, education, and income levels. How can churches address their contexts and still be united in Christ?

7. What are the privileges and status that you and your church enjoy?

8. Can or should The United Methodist Church give more space to traditionalists and progressives? How might that look in your local situation?

9. How does context change ministry?

10. If space and relationship are not opposites as Bishop Schnase suggests, how can we live into the tension they create in the local church? In your annual conference? In The United Methodist Church?

11. Discuss this statement found in the Nicene Creed (#880 in the UM Hymnal): "We believe in the one, holy, catholic, and apostolic church." In the creed what do "one," "holy," "catholic," and "apostolic" mean?

12. How do bishops give visible expression to the oneness of the church?

13. How do churches give visible expression to the Methodist connection?

14. If you knew you could not fail and had all power of heaven on your side, how would you engage the edges and multiply your witness? Make a list and start engaging.

7

Engage
for Generous Orthodoxy, United Methodism, and the Missio Dei in the United States

Kenneth H. Carter Jr.
Resident Bishop of the Florida Episcopal Area,
The United Methodist Church, and a Moderator
of the Commission on a Way Forward

I have an increasing clarity about a Christian faith that is *generously orthodox*. The word *orthodox*, as used here, has a distinctively lower case "o." It is about my trust in the scriptures, the creeds, and the faith of the church. I am carried along by a great current of Christian tradition that is deep and wide, ecumenical and global, Trinitarian and liberationist.[1] It is a faith that articulates the cries of God's people (Ex. 3), that breathes life into a valley of dry bones (Ezek. 37), that endures weeping in the night but awakens to a joy that comes in the morning (Ps. 30). It wanders in the wilderness (Ex. 16), experiences the dark night of the soul (Ps. 22), knows a peace that surpasses human understanding (Phil. 4), and discovers the empty tomb (John 20).

---

1 For the significance of both/and I am indebted to Paul Chilcote, *Recapturing the Wesleys' Vision* (Downer's Grove, IL: InterVarsity Academic Press, 2004).

The word *generous* is about charity toward others in the body of Christ, patience with them in their own spiritual journeys, openness to the possibility that we see through a glass darkly (1 Cor. 13), and humility that we consider others more highly than we do ourselves (Phil. 2). Generosity creates a space for reciprocity, giving, and receiving. Generosity acknowledges a dark side to orthodoxy, one that draws too sharp a division and too strong a boundary, one that can be related to power and privilege, and in the process people who worship, pray, learn, serve, and witness together are separated (literally torn apart, in the Greek *skhizein*, schism).

The phrase "generous orthodoxy" was coined by the Yale theologian Hans Frei a generation ago and influenced a number of his students, many of whom would later teach at Duke, where I studied. Frei commented that "we need a kind of generous orthodoxy which would have in it an element of liberalism—a voice like the *Christian Century*—and an element of evangelicalism—the voice of *Christianity Today*. I don't know if there is a voice between these two, as a matter of fact. If there is, I would like to pursue it."[2]

Generous Orthodoxy is the title of a blog by the brilliant Episcopal preacher and priest Fleming Rutledge, who writes,

> We cannot do without orthodoxy, for everything else must be tested against it, but that orthodox (traditional, classical) Christian faith should by definition always be generous as our God is generous; lavish in his creation, binding himself in an unconditional covenant, revealing himself in the calling of a people, self-sacrificing in the death of his Son, prodigal in the gifts of the Spirit, justifying the ungodly and, indeed, offending the "righteous" by the indiscriminate use of his favor. True Christian orthodoxy therefore cannot be narrow,

---

2 Hans Frei, "Response to Narrative Theology: An Evangelical Appraisal," *Trinity Journal*, Spring 1987.

pinched or defensive but [is] always spacious, adventurous
and unafraid.[3]

More recently, "Generous Orthodoxy" is the title of a podcast
by Malcolm Gladwell (Revisionist History), in telling the story of a
same-gender wedding in the Mennonite Church tradition, and how
that community navigated the claims of received truth and expressed
conscience. The story itself is narrated in a gracious way, especially
given the medium of popular culture. In his own reflection on the
events narrated in the podcast, Gladwell notes that "you must respect
the body you are trying to heal."[4]

What great things God could accomplish if we rediscovered an orthodoxy in service of the healing (and not dividing) of our bodies, that
is, our churches![5] Such a generous orthodoxy would help prevent us
from becoming immersed in the emotional processes that pit people
against one another. Such a generous orthodoxy would keep us from
becoming stuck in cycles of harmful collusion and escalating conflict.[6]
Such a generous orthodoxy would know that the source of our capacity to be healed of our schisms is a miracle beyond our human power
or goodness or intelligence.

I do empathize with those who do not see or hold the faith as I do.
My way is not the superior way or the only way. I do believe, however,

---

3 Fleming Rutledge, "What is generous orthodoxy? A statement of purpose," accessed
   March 22, 2018, www.generousorthodoxy.org.

4 "Generous Orthodoxy" Season 1, episode 9, of podcast *Revisionist History*, accessed March
   22, 2018, http://revisionisthistory.com/episodes/09-generous-orthodoxy.

5 I am aware of public responses to my recent reflection on generous orthodoxy by David
   Watson (https://davidfwatson.me/2017/08/15/the-innate-generosity-of-orthodoxy/ and
   Joel Watts (http://unsettledchristianity.com/generous-orthodoxy-reply-bishop-carter/). I
   share their defense of a high Christology and appreciation of the great tradition; I respect-
   fully differ in seeking to channel more of my energies in defining an orthodoxy that is
   generous in the pursuit of the unity of the church.

6 See The Arbinger Institute, *The Anatomy of Peace: Resolving the Heart of Conflict* (Oak-
   land, CA: Berrett-Koehler, 2006). This has been a primary text of the Commission on a Way
   Forward of The United Methodist Church.

because of experiences, teachers, relationships, and vocational calling that this is the way God has given me to walk. Because my faith is orthodox, I can learn from and listen to voices many would characterize as moderate, evangelical, catholic, and traditional. These theological streams have always been life-giving to me.[7]

Because my faith is generously orthodox, I believe that the heart and soul of orthodoxy is grace. This grace is a broad, deep river, a wide reservoir of divine love, a fountain filled with blood that has the power to overcome all of my resistance and rebellion. It is a grace greater than all my sin. And this grace is for all people. Note the words of Charles Wesley:

> Teach me to cast my net aright,
>> The gospel net of general grace,
> So shall I *all* to Thee invite,
>> And draw them to their Lord's embrace,
> Within Thine arms of love include,
>> And catch a willing multitude.[8]

Note the prominence of the word *all* throughout the body of Charles Wesley's hymns, for example:

> "Jesus, thou art *all* compassion";
> "God hath bid *all* humankind";
> "truth and love let *all* men see";
> "to me, to *all*, thy mercies move";
> "O may we *all* the loving mind that was in thee receive."

Because grace is for all, a generous orthodoxy knows that God can never be tribal. The God of the Bible, the God of the Old and New Covenants, is never tribal. From Abraham to Ruth to Isaiah to Jesus and

---

7 For the imagery of streams of theological tradition, see Thomas A. Langford, *Practical Divinity: Theology in the Wesleyan Tradition, Volume One* (Nashville: Abingdon Press, 1998).

8 Chilcote, *Recapturing the Wesleys' Vision*, 98.

Paul and the Revelation given to John, the tribal is always an interim form of community on the way to something greater that God is wanting to do. At our best, and at our most biblical, we know this.

Please hear this confession less as an attempt to spin something politically and more as a statement of faith. I have been formed by Sunday school teachers and hymns, seminary professors and books, my conversion and baptism, family and missionaries, pastors and activists, by friends much more conservative and much more liberal than I will ever be. I simply refuse to give in to the idea that Christian faith and practice in the United States must conform to the same political and cultural boxes that divide us so profoundly. I push back against some of those assumptions and some of the ways we label each other. Generosity persuades me to believe that the Church (The United Methodist Church, the ecumenical church, your church and my church, the church that will be recreated by the generations coming along) has a better and more faithful future. This is the work of a God who is creating, redeeming, and sanctifying us.

I am not naive about nor oblivious to our divisions. For this reason the missio Dei in the United States requires careful, patient, and substantive attention to the reconciliation of the broken body of Christ, as a sign and witness of our profession of "one Lord, one faith, one baptism, one God and Father of all" (Eph. 4:5-6, NRSV). This is the basis of our hope for a church that does not merely reflect the cultural and political divisions of the United States but bears witness to a deeper identity, one expressed in the latter half of Ephesians 2.

At the level of practice I am drawn to the gift and challenge of Matthew 18, which has been a resource in the covenantal life of the Commission on a Way Forward.[9] Our experience of escalating ecclesial conflict might look very different if we were discipled in the way of

---

9   The covenant, adopted by the thirty-two commissioners from four continents, is posted here: http://www.umc.org/who-we-are/commission-on-a-way-forward-about-us.

Jesus: "If another member of the church sins against you, go and point out the fault when the two of you are alone. If the member listens to you, you have regained that one. But if you are not listened to, take one or two others along with you, so that every word may be confirmed by the evidence of two or three witnesses" (Matt. 18:15-16, NRSV).

Stanley Hauerwas has reflected on this text as a resource that might lead us to confession, forgiveness, and reconciliation. He observes, "That conflict is a part and parcel of Christian unity means that the unity of a church is not a unity based on agreements, but rather one that assumes that disagreements should not lead to division but rather should be a testimony to the existence of a reconciling people."[10]

What if orthodoxy is not the elimination of our differences but the calling to live together faithfully in the midst of them? In seeking to visualize what a generous orthodoxy might look like, in practice, I have used a simple drawing of three circles to portray something of where we are as a Church in the present moment.[11]

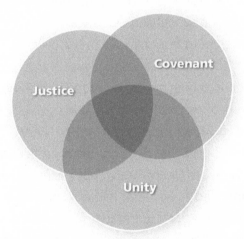

---

10 "Which Church? What Unity? or An Attempt to Say What I May Think about the Future of Christian Unity" in *Approaching the End: Eschatological Reflections on Church, Politics, and Life* (Grand Rapids, MI: Eerdmans, 2013), 109.

11 From Kenneth H. Carter Jr., "Remembering Who We Are: Where Covenant, Justice, and Unity Meet," *Ministry Matters*, October 19, 2017, http://www.ministrymatters.com/all/entry/8479/remembering-who-we-are-where-covenant-justice-and-unity-meet.

The three circles are covenant, justice, and unity; and I visualize them as coming together to create an overlapping space, not unlike a Venn diagram.[12]

Covenantal people greatly value the promises we have made to God and to one another in baptism, in ordination, and in consecration. They seek greater public accountability when our covenants are broken.

Those in a search for justice participate in a history that gives greater rights and offers God's grace and blessings to more people. This history includes the abolition of slavery, the recognition of women in ministry, and now the inclusion of the LGBTQI community in the full life of the church.

Those who value unity have the conviction that covenantal people and justice seekers can live together in the church. They do not see the present LGBTQI conversation as a church-dividing issue; and they live in the tension, often at the congregational level, amidst differences that reflect the beauty and complexity of the one body.

My own calling is to seek to expand or grow the space where these three circles overlap. I share passions of justice, covenant, and unity with friends across my own annual conference and the global Church. The shared space where justice, covenant, and unity overlap is not a mushy middle! It is the complex place where many faithful people live. It is the practical divinity that flows from a generous orthodoxy. It is more closely aligned with Bishop Scott Jones's image of an "extreme center."[13]

The vision of the Commission on a Way Forward is to "design a way for being church that maximizes the presence of a United Methodist witness in as many places in the world as possible, that allows for

---

12 For a definition and picture of a Venn diagram, see https://en.wikipedia.org/wiki/Venn _diagram.

13 Scott J. Jones, *United Methodist Doctrine: The Extreme Center* (Nashville: Abingdon Press, 2002).

as much contextual differentiation as possible, and that balances an approach to different theological understandings of human sexuality with a desire for as much unity as possible."[14]

I understand this to be the generative work of our denomination in this present moment. And this generative work is possible through the theological resources of a generous orthodoxy.

In his *Recapturing the Wesleys' Vision*, Paul Chilcote describes our tradition as a "place" that is not "either/or" but "both/and." "The Wesleyan method," he writes, "can be called conjunctive because it seeks to join things together, rather than permitting them to be pulled apart."[15] And so he speaks of faith and works, personal and social, heart and head, Christ and culture, piety and mercy.

This is The United Methodist Church in its most local and global expression. At our best we are connected to each other for a purpose: "to make disciples of Jesus Christ for the transformation of the world" (*The Book of Discipline*, 121). This mission includes keeping covenant, loving justice, and seeking unity. And it is about growing, expanding, and honoring the space where these three values can be joined together.

The recovery of a generously orthodox faith matters. When we are generous, we are not closed off from one another. This is for our good. When we are orthodox, we are not separated from the God who speaks, is incarnate, and breathes in scripture and in our own lives. This is our salvation. As Fleming Rutledge states on her blog *Generous Orthodoxy*, this is the Church's mission that is "spacious, adventurous, and unafraid." If we know the history of how God has moved for millennia over the face of this creation, why would we imagine that the renewal, reform, and healing of the church would not be a recovery of how we think about God and how we therefore live in transformed ways with one another? And if we were reading the signs

---

14 This can be accessed at http://www.umc.org/who-we-are/commission-on-a-way-forward -about-us.

15 Chilcote, *Recapturing the Wesleys' Vision*, 16.

of the times, why would we not trust that this same God was and is in Christ reconciling the world to God's self, and that God has given us—The United Methodist Church planted on US soil—this ministry of reconciliation (2 Cor. 5)?[16]

Questions for Discussion

1. Bishop Carter says: "The word *orthodox*, as used here, has a distinctively lower case 'o.' It is about my trust in the scriptures, the creeds, and the faith of the church." How do you understand "orthodoxy"? Take a moment to read and reflect on some of our creeds found in the back of *The United Methodist Hymnal*.

2. For Bishop Carter, being generous involves offering charity, especially as charity is described in 1 Corinthians 13. In some translations, the Greek word *agape* is translated as "love" and in others as "charity." How might our church, our denomination, be different if we practiced charity/love? How can generosity heal the wounds of conflict in our family, church, and denomination?

3. What might it mean to say that God is generous? Share an experience of God's generosity. How does God's generosity differ from human generosity? How can we demonstrate God's generosity to others?

4. Looking at the diagram of the three intersecting circles, in which circle do you feel most comfortable: covenant, justice, or unity? Bishop Carter calls the intersection the "extreme center."

5. What words would you use to describe the intersection of covenant, justice, and unity?

6. United Methodists believe in faith and works, personal and social,

---

16 For this reason the work of reconciliation—among races, across economic lines, amidst theological differences, with persons of LGBTQI identity—is not an interruption or obstacle to our mission; these may be critical teaching contexts that cry out for the deep resources and convictions of biblical faith and Wesleyan tradition.

heart and head, Christ and culture, piety and mercy. What are the strengths and weaknesses of practicing a both/and faith? Give some examples of living into the tension of believing in both faith and works, personal and social responsibility, and a heart and head religion.

7. If our church's mission is to be "spacious, adventurous, and unafraid," what steps should we take now?

8. If you were certain that all power of heaven and earth was on your side and that you could not fail, in what mission would you engage? What dreams would you dream for our church? Make a list and start making those dreams come true.

CPSIA information can be obtained
at www.ICGtesting.com
Printed in the USA
BVHW07s1631210518
516872BV00007B/597/P